D0882868

Oct/Nov
2004

	NOV 1 9 2004
1011	

BRODART, CO.   Cat. No. 23-221-003

THIS BOOK BELONGS TO THE
VAN BUREN PUBLIC LIBRARY

Murder at Mount Hermon

Murder
at Mount Hermon

❧

The Unsolved Killing of
Headmaster Elliott Speer

CRAIG WALLEY

Northeastern University Press
BOSTON

Northeastern University Press

Copyright 2004 by Craig Walley

All rights reserved. Except for the quotation of short passages for the purposes of criticism and review, no part of this book may be reproduced in any form or by any means, electronic or mechanical, including photocopying, recording, or any information storage and retrieval system now known or to be invented, without written permission of the publisher.

Library of Congress Cataloging-in-Publication Data

Walley, Craig, 1943–
Murder at Mount Hermon : the unsolved killing of headmaster Elliott Speer /
Craig Walley.
p.   cm.
Includes index.
ISBN 1-55553-618-2 (cloth : alk. paper)
1. Speer, Elliott, d. 1934. 2. Mount Hermon School for Boys.
3. Murder—Massachusetts—History—Case studies.
4. School principals—Crimes against—Massachusetts—History—Case studies.
5. Murder—Investigation—Massachusetts—History—Case studies. I. Title.
HV6533.M4W36   2004
364.152′3′0974422—dc22   2004001097

Designed by Janis Owens, Books By Design, Inc.

Composed in Fairfield Medium by Coghill Composition Company in Richmond, Virginia.
Printed and bound by Maple Press in York, Pennsylvania. The paper is Maple Tradebook,
an acid-free sheet.

MANUFACTURED IN THE UNITED STATES OF AMERICA
08   07   06   05   04   5   4   3   2   1

To the memory of my parents

Contents

❧⋅❧

Illustrations

Preface

❦❦

I attended Mount Hermon School from 1957 to 1961. In those days, we ate at assigned tables in West Hall, and a faculty member always joined us for lunch. Sometime during those years, one of those faculty members told us about the murder of Headmaster Elliott Speer in 1934. This was much more interesting than the usual lunch conversation; after all, we could see the site of the crime, Ford Cottage, from the south end of West Hall, and if we went to Ford Cottage, we could also see the holes in the wall of the study said to have been made by the shotgun slugs that had missed Elliott Speer a quarter of a century before. No one had been charged with the crime. I remembered the story and was always anxious to learn more about this mystery.

College, law school, a family, and a legal career followed, and though I was still involved, at least emotionally, with Mount Hermon, I forgot about the headmaster's murder. An article in *Yankee* magazine by Burnham Carter in October 1977, however, rekindled my interest. Carter had been a classmate of Elliott Speer at Princeton and was writing a book about the murder, to be titled *The Devil's Chapel*. The article described his search for sources of information about the killing, including the transcripts of the secret inquest held in December 1934.

After that, I regularly checked the library for this promised new book. It was not until 1981, while I was attending our class's twentieth reunion, that I learned that Carter had died before he could finish the book. The faculty member who told me this said that he was thinking about writing the story himself. So again, I waited to have someone else tell me the details: Why had the headmaster been killed? Why had no one been convicted or even charged with the killing?

Another reunion arrived—in 2001—and, with it, another chance to air out that old memory and find out who was going to solve the mystery for me. During a reception on the lawn south of Ford Cottage, the faculty member who had said twenty years before that he was thinking about writing the book told me that he was no longer going to do it. I wondered if I would ever have a chance to learn more about this murder.

Before the reunion, the very efficient staff at the school (now called Northfield Mount Hermon School, Mount Hermon having merged with its sister school in 1971) sent out a booklet containing schedules, dormitory assignments, and special events for alumni. One of the options available was a visit to the school archives. The booklet said that the archivist, Peter Weis, would welcome visits from the alumni during certain hours. My wife, always more diligent than I, was reviewing the booklet (even though she was not going to attend the reunion) and noticed Peter's name. We knew Peter—he had married a young woman artist we had met—and they had visited us in Columbus. I agreed with my wife that I would drop in and say hello.

Having learned that no one was working on the Speer murder, I had another purpose for visiting Peter beyond renewing our friendship. I found the archives on the lower floor of the modern brick library on the Northfield campus. Peter welcomed me, and I asked him what he had on the Speer murder. "Lots," he said. He took me into the back room and showed me the file boxes. Not only was there a nearly complete transcript of the inquest, but the boxes also held a transcript of a preliminary hearing in the 1937 assault case against Dean Elder, letters of condolence from September 1934, and records of the memorial services for Elliott Speer. On the shelves were albums of news clippings. I sat down at the round table in the archives with the inquest transcript and read the crucial testimony of Wilfred Fry. I was hooked. Over the next year, I was to spend many happy hours in Peter's archives.

Many others contributed to my research. I had the pleasure of meeting—in person, over the telephone, by e-mail, or by regular mail—many who had been at the school or had been involved in the investigations. Elliott Speer's oldest daughter, Carrie, who had looked down the stairwell in Ford Cottage on the night of September 14, 1934, and seen her father dying in her mother's arms, was generous with her time and memories and put me in touch with others who could help. Dr. William Cole, class of 1935, who had preached in Memorial Chapel in my student days, graciously shared his recollections of Elliott Speer and Mount Hermon. Edwin "Red" Thompson, class of 1934, had been asked by the investigators to return to campus after the killing and meet with Dean Elder to prepare a list of former students who might have grudges against Speer. He was tremendously helpful to me, offering anecdotes and insights and kindly correcting errors in the manuscript that I sent him. Prestley Blake of the class of 1935 was also an enthusiastic supporter of my efforts, as was Richard Gale of the class of 1941, who had worked at the school beginning in the 1930s. Many of these kind people read portions of this book and corrected many of my errors. Those that remain are my responsibility.

The current headmaster, Richard Mueller, and his charming wife Claire were consistently enthusiastic about the project. Richard, in spite of a very busy schedule, took time to bring me up to date on developments at the school. Claire gave me a full tour of Ford Cottage, including, of course, the study where Speer was shot (which still serves as a study), the upstairs bedroom where Holly Speer heard the shot, and the hallway where Elliott Speer died.

I also want to thank the editors at Northeastern University Press, particularly Sarah Rowley and Emily McKeigue, for their support and kindness. For work on the illustrations and maps, thanks go to Jim Hager of Renovo Media.

It is traditional to thank members of the writer's family—if only to keep peace. But in this case, my wife Connie and my son Jonathan not only bore with patience my endless ruminations about the project, but also read various versions of it and offered thoughtful and helpful suggestions, always remaining careful to protect the writer's fragile ego. Connie is a fine and patient editor, as well as a matchless wife. Jonathan also arranged to have the Pathé News newsreel film concerning the inquest transferred to video.

Murder at Mount Hermon

Prologue:
The Key to Heaven

October 30, 1932

Mount Hermon School for Boys
Mount Hermon, Massachusetts

It was a time of change in the United States. On the national scene
the voters were about to end twelve years of Republican domi-
nance and elect a dynamic, liberal Franklin D. Roosevelt to replace
the staid, conservative Herbert Hoover.

On a smaller stage, a ceremony at this small private secondary
school in northern Massachusetts echoed the same theme. Henry
Cutler, who had been headmaster for more than forty years, was
retiring. Stocky and fit at age seventy, he had been considered progressive in his early years, but for more than a decade the school
had stood still as the world changed. Although many in the faculty
and administration were comfortable with the rigid rules—no card
playing, no newspapers on Sunday, no classes on Monday (so the
students would not be tempted to read works other than the Bible,
or to study, on the Sabbath)—younger members of the faculty and

3

the board of trustees believed that change was needed. They turned to the president of the board, thirty-three-year-old Elliott Speer. Lanky and athletic, Speer was physically a sharp contrast to Cutler, but the two were friends and Speer was Cutler's choice to succeed him. This was the day Speer was to be installed in his new position.

The installation ceremony in the school's Memorial Chapel was attended by members of the student body, faculty, and administration. Among those present was Wilfred Fry, who was replacing Speer as president of the board. The handsome Fry was a successful and wealthy businessman and supporter of the school. Trustee John Grandin, a plainspoken businessman from Boston, was also on hand. Among the faculty present was William Morrow—one of the young ones and an avid bridge player. He was sure that Speer would allow bridge, since he knew that the new headmaster was a player himself.

Sitting near the new headmaster, the school chaplain Lester White knew that Speer would liberalize the religious program at the school, and he looked forward to the changes. Similarly, Rich-

Headmaster Elliott Speer and Dean Thomas Elder. Courtesy of Northfield Mount Hermon School archives.

ard Watson, a fireplug of a man, known affectionately by the students as "King Watson," was ready to support Speer, as he had supported Dr. Cutler for more years than anyone could remember. At this time, he was superintendent of buildings.

Watson's friend Tom Elder, though, opposed change for personal reasons. Cutler had made him dean, or second-in-command (and, Elder had thought, successor-designate). Elder had loyally supported the old headmaster. He did not welcome the installation of a thirty-three-year-old to succeed Cutler, and he recognized that his chance of being promoted to headmaster was gone unless Speer's term should end prematurely.

At the end of his speech welcoming Speer as the new headmaster, Fry used the key to Ford Cottage—the headmaster's residence—as a symbol of the headmaster's position, and said he hoped it would also be the key to the hearts of the faculty and students. Accepting the key, Speer responded, "Thank you Mr. President, for this key. If it be, as you say, the key to Ford Cottage, and also the key to all these hearts, may it not also be possibly a key to Heaven?"

Murder at Ford Cottage

❦

Friday, September 14, 1934

Mount Hermon School for Boys
Mount Hermon, Massachusetts

The campus lay quiet in the evening. The fall term, the beginning of a new school year, would begin the following week. The nearly empty red brick dormitories and classroom buildings had been cleaned and painted during the summer. The school bookstore was stuffed with its inventory of textbooks. The faculty and their families had returned from their summer vacations. And thirty-five "old boys" who would be starting their junior and senior years had returned to campus early to help prepare the school for the new term and to greet the rest of the students who would begin arriving Monday.

After dinner in West Hall, most of the old boys were attending a meeting with one of the teachers in four-story Crossley Hall, the newest and largest dormitory on the campus.

Elliott Speer, the youthful headmaster, his wife Charlotte,

6

Crossley Hall is the school's largest building. West Hall (the dining hall) is in the upper right side of the picture. Ford Cottage is just out of the picture, on the right. Memorial Chapel with its clock tower (above West Hall and a little to the left) is separated from Crossley by Cottage Row. Holbrook Hall (administration) is on the upper left edge of the photograph. Courtesy of Northfield Mount Hermon School archives.

whom everyone called "Holly," and their three daughters, Caroline, twelve, Eleanor, ten, and Margaret, four, had returned earlier in the week. They had spent most of the summer building a cabin on an island in Lake Timagami in northern Canada. The headmaster and his family lived in Ford Cottage, a large brick Georgian-style house a hundred yards south of West Hall. After dinner with his family and his wife's parents, Mr. and Mrs. Henry Welles, who were visiting, Speer, as was his habit, walked across the hall to his study to review the accumulated paperwork and prepare for the coming term.

*Ford Cottage. The headmaster's study is on the ground floor on the
northeast corner—the far right side of the building in this
photograph—with windows on the front and side.
The shot was fired through the window
on the north side. Author's photo.*

Elliott Speer was excited about the future—he looked forward
to the return of the old students and the welcoming of the new.
He was also anticipating with pleasure teaching a course this
year—a welcome break from the administrative duties of the headmaster's job.

It was a little after eight o'clock in the evening when he sat
down at his desk in the study. During the day there was a fine view
to the east from the window to his right. Beyond the trees in front
of the house stood the solid gray stone chapel just down the hill;
beyond it stood the gymnasium, with its Greek-style columns, and
beyond that the rest of the campus sloping down to the Connecticut River. The hills on the far side of the gentle valley were a green
and brown quilt of woods, pastures, and fields at this time of the
year. In the September mornings, fog formed along the river and
then rose and was dispersed in the warmth of the sun, revealing

the changing colors of the New England autumn. In the evening, the setting sun reddened the hillsides across the river.

Looking north out the window in front of his desk during the day, Elliott Speer could see West Hall through the small maple tree in front of the window and, just to the east, a neat row of five brick cottages—called "Cottage Row"—which were the oldest dormitories on the campus. He could also see the tops of the elms that lined the walkway from the cottages to the classroom buildings. Crossley Hall was out of sight beyond.

The main campus of Mount Hermon described a large irregular rectangle of widely spaced buildings reflecting the various architectural styles of the previous fifty years, along with their surrounding terraced lawns, trees, and athletic fields. The chapel, the five cottages, West Hall, and Crossley made up the western side, on the high ground. East of Crossley, down the hill, stood the library and Holbrook Hall (the administration building), which housed the headmaster's and the dean's offices. The eastern side of the rectangle included classroom buildings and the gymnasium; it ended at an old brick dormitory, Overtoun Hall, on the southeast corner. Back up the hill from Overtoun were some faculty homes, the chapel, sitting on an outcrop of New England granite, and, behind the chapel, on the highest point, Ford Cottage. Behind Ford Cottage was a grove of pine trees that had been planted in the 1920s as a memorial to the alumni who had died in World War I. Acres of dense maple and oak woods stood beyond the pine trees.

That evening it was dark and cloudy, and Elliott Speer could not see outside the window as he sat at his well-lighted desk, surrounded by his books, preparing for the new term. In the darkness of that September evening, among the branches of the maple tree a few yards from the headmaster, stood someone else, watching Speer through the window. He carried a 12-gauge shotgun loaded with double-o buckshot. No doubt he, too, was feeling excitement and anticipation as he raised the gun and aimed it slightly upward through the high window. He waited until the tall headmaster stood to reach for a book in the bookshelves next to his desk.

The nine double-o slugs tore through the screen and the win-

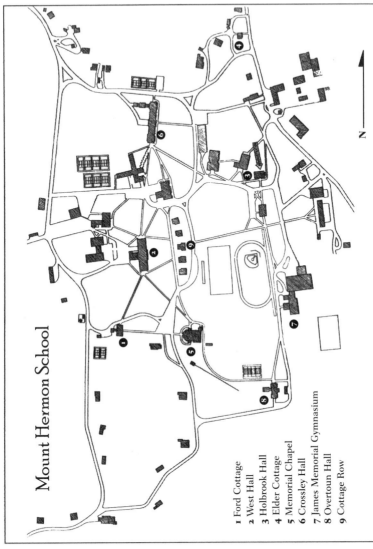

Map of the school in Speer's day. Courtesy of Northfield Mount Hermon School archives.

Mount Hermon School

1 Ford Cottage
2 West Hall
3 Holbrook Hall
4 Elder Cottage
5 Memorial Chapel
6 Crossley Hall
7 James Memorial Gymnasium
8 Overtoun Hall
9 Cottage Row

dow before reaching Speer's right side. Eight hit him in the shoulder and the chest. One of them pierced his heart.

Holly was upstairs with her mother, in the bedroom directly over her husband's study, when she heard the shot and the shattering of glass. She thought at first that a light bulb had exploded, but when she came down the staircase to check, she was met by her bleeding husband, who had staggered into the hall. "I don't know

The Speer family shortly before Elliott's murder.
Back row left to right: Caroline, Holly, and
Elliott. Front row left to right: Margaret
and Eleanor. Courtesy of Northfield
Mount Hermon School archives.

what happened," he said. Holly and her father, who had rushed
out of the drawing room just across the hall, caught him as he
collapsed and lowered him to the floor. Holly sat on the first step
of the stairway and supported her barely conscious husband.

Florence George, the Speers' maid, also heard the shot and
then the sound of "quick running steps" heading north and east—
toward the road that passes in front of the cottages. At the same

time, Daniel Bodley, head of the school's laundry, and William Dierig, who ran the school's carpentry shop, and their wives were standing near the post office just north of Cottage Row, approximately 200 yards north of Ford Cottage. They, too, heard a sound they thought was either a shot—"someone killing a skunk"—or a car's backfire. They did not give it much thought. Shortly after, they noticed a car that had passed them a few minutes before headed in the direction of Ford Cottage. Now it sped in front of Cottage Row, passed by them quickly, and turned toward Crossley and the exit from the campus. Bodley remembered that the car was a dark sedan, possibly a boxy Franklin, several years old.

Back at Ford Cottage, Holly, her father, and the servants attempted to help the dying headmaster. They summoned a doctor from nearby Greenfield and David Birdsall, who lived on campus nearby. Birdsall and his wife were close friends of the Speers—and "Uncle David and Aunt Sophie" to the Speer children. Birdsall drove the short distance to the headmaster's house. It was so dark that he tripped over a small hedge in front of the building when he jumped out of his old Plymouth coupe.

The doctor was the next to arrive. He recognized quickly that there was no hope for the unconscious headmaster. "He was beyond aid when I got there." Elliott Speer died at 8:55 P.M.

David Birdsall had called the police, and they arrived about an hour after the shot had been fired. Sophie Birdsall had by now run over from her house and was sitting on the stairs next to Holly. Shortly after the police arrived, the school's dean, Thomas Elder, called Ford Cottage asking to speak to Elliott. At first, Holly's father—aware that Elder suffered from heart problems and not wanting to upset him—told him only that the headmaster could not come to the telephone. But Elder insisted on speaking to Speer, and Mr. Welles finally told him of the shooting. Elder drove from Holbrook Hall, where he had been working, up to Ford Cottage, and then began calling the school's trustees to inform them of the murder.

Numb, Holly Speer sat on the stairs in the broad center hallway, holding her dead husband's hand. When Dean Elder urged her to go upstairs and rest, she said quietly, "No, I don't feel as though I should ever leave this spot." She turned to Sophie and asked, "What shall I do?" Sophie said, "If that's what you want to do, I should stay right here."

Finally, when Elliott Speer's body had been taken away, she agreed to rest, but not before supervising the cleaning of the hall. She did not want the children to be confronted with bloodstains when they came downstairs in the morning.

2

Mount Hermon from Moody to Speer

Elliott Speer had already accomplished much in the two years since he had assumed the headmaster's job. Tall and youthful, he had quickly captured the affection and loyalty of the students with his charm, his progressive ideas, and his sense of humor. He had begun modernizing the school and its curriculum and improving the quality of the faculty. At the same time, he maintained the traditions of religious training and respect for physical labor established by the school's founder, the evangelist Dwight L. Moody.

Moody, known as "D. L." by generations of Mount Hermon students, was in a sense the embodiment of the nineteenth-century American success story. One of nine children, he was born in 1837 into a modest farm family in rural East Northfield, Massachusetts. With little schooling, but with a warm personality and ambition, he left home at seventeen and became a successful shoe salesman, first in Boston and then in Chicago. While in Boston he was, as he put it, "converted." Words from a Sunday School teacher (adults more commonly attended Sunday School at that time) had moved Moody to become an active and committed Christian. He soon gave up the shoe business and by the end of the Civil War was becoming one of the best-known evangelists in the country. He won over his audiences with his hearty, uncomplicated enthusiasm. He preached a gospel of God's love and joy. He was not a theologian, and he did not believe in threatening unrepentant sinners with hellfire and brimstone. "Terror never brought a man in yet," he said. Moody never took a salary for his religious work, and there was never a whiff of scandal about him. A measure of his popularity is the fact that the hymnal that he and his musician partner, Ira Sankey, authored sold 70 million copies.

Given his background, it is not surprising that when Moody founded the Northfield Seminary and Mount Hermon, he stipulated that they were for poor girls and boys and that the focus of the schools was to be Christian education. (The boys' school was named for Mount Hermon in biblical Israel, referred to in Psalm 133, verse 3: "As the dew of Hermon, and as the dew that descended upon the mountains of Zion: for there the Lord commanded the blessing, even life for evermore.") He wanted these young people to have the educational opportunity that he had lacked, but he believed that education without a moral component was dangerous. "An educated rascal," he said, "is worse than a rascal."

When Speer began his term as headmaster in 1932, the rules and routine at Mount Hermon had hardly changed from the time Moody had founded it in 1881. During the 1880s, less than 10 percent of high-school-age students in the United States attended school. College then was the realm of the privileged, and Mount Hermon's curriculum was not primarily designed to prepare students for college. Moody had created the schools to provide educational opportunities for children of poor families and to train them to be morally strong Christians who would be successful in the secular world—becoming "spokesmen for Christ" in their workaday lives.

Henry Cutler, who had been headmaster since 1890, was not primarily interested in the religious aspects of the school and had worked to improve the academic side. But during his long tenure as headmaster, the world changed fundamentally, while the school's religious practices and beliefs did not. William Compton, a former faculty member and acute observer of the school's religious life later reflected:

> What was right and proper in 1890 was anachronistic in 1930. Those years witnessed a profound upheaval in American protestantism and the struggle between traditionalists who took the words of the bible literally, and modernists who accepted Darwin's theory of evolution and the historical interpretations of biblical texts. The 1920s witnessed dramatic battles between these two forces, most notably in the Scopes trial. At Mount Hermon, Cutler managed to dodge a direct confrontation by focusing on accepting Christ as the key and letting both fundamentalists and modernists teach on the faculty.

Of course, "modern thinking" affected far more than religion. By the time Elliott Speer became Mount Hermon's headmaster, World War I, the Russian Revolution, and the stock market crash of 1929 had altered the worldview of all thinking people. Einstein, Freud, Marx, and others provided new intellectual foundations for understanding humanity and the world. The hiring of Speer, first as president of both schools in 1927, and then as Mount Hermon's headmaster, signaled that the board of trustees was determined on a course of modernization. The fact that Elliott Speer was an ordained minister, however, demonstrated that the religious tradition of the schools would not be abandoned.

Reflecting the revolution in the intellectual and economic realms, manners and morals had also changed in the half-century since Moody had founded Mount Hermon. But in 1932 the campus was still in the grip of conservative traditionalists, bound to preserve this remnant of New England Puritanism. They were increasingly out of step with the rest of society. Even faculty members could not smoke, the students could not read newspapers on Sunday, and owning a deck of cards was cause for expulsion. And despite the proximity of the five hundred young women of the Northfield Seminary, operated jointly with Mount Hermon, there was almost no social contact between the sexes. The only exception was the "parlor date" on Monday afternoons, in which students of the two schools could meet in the parlor of the girls' dormitory and chat over tea or punch, closely chaperoned by members of the faculty. Since no transportation was provided, even in the bitter New England winters, the boys had to walk to the North-field campus for these dates. "Two miles over and ten back," they said. William Cole, a graduate, described Mount Hermon in the early 1930s as "like Brigadoon—lost in the mists of the nineteenth century." Elliott Speer blew the mist away.

In the two years of his headmastership, Speer, with the blessing of the trustees, liberalized the social program, even allowing dances for the boys of Mount Hermon and the young ladies of the Northfield Seminary. In fact, he hired teachers from the Arthur Murray Dance Studios in New York to tutor the students in the terpsichorean arts. The girls from the seminary were bused to Mount Hermon, and the lessons were held in the gymnasium. On one occasion, after teaching the students the rudiments of the waltz, the Arthur Murray teacher (remembered as "stunningly beautiful") explained dancing etiquette—"On the dance floor, well, just dance." She told the students that the girl should maintain a dance position far enough away from the boy that he could not step on her feet. She invited Mr. Speer—the tallest man in the room—to dance with her and try to step on her feet. Laughing, he tried, but even with his long legs he could not. The school newspaper, *The Hermonite*, dryly noted, "After sufficiently mastering [the waltz], the students were taught some essential ballroom etiquette; Mr. Speer is to be congratulated for the noble part that he played in this particular demonstration."

An avid bridge player, Speer quickly discarded the prohibition against card playing, which had applied even to the faculty. Bill Morrow, a younger member of the faculty at that period, recalled the welcome change: "No longer did Anne [Morrow's wife] and I and others have to play bridge behind drawn shades or locked doors with a Parcheesi board nearby to cover the bridge hands in case a visitor came a-knocking."

At the same time, Elliott Speer began raising academic standards and improving the faculty, even hiring graduates of the progressive Union Theological Seminary to revitalize the antiquated Bible Department. He also allowed interscholastic athletic competition. These changes—although welcomed wholeheartedly by the students and most of the faculty as long overdue—brought protests, sometimes passionate, from older alumni and conservative members of the faculty. One alumnus, Reverend Samuel McDowell, wrote to protest the headmaster's decision to allow dancing: "Our young people do not know the evil nor damning consequences of the modern dance. . . . Many an innocent, pure, fine, noble girl has gone . . . to the dance floor not knowing the peril of it, and has come out a physical and moral wreck, with hopes blighted, virtue stolen, prospects clouded, and womanhood gone." Nevertheless, Speer was encouraged and confident that he was doing the right thing for the school.

At age thirty-four, Speer was one of the youngest headmasters in the country and already a respected educator. In 1927, only six years out of Princeton, he had been named president of the two schools, and the faith of the schools' trustees in the youthful Speer had not wavered, despite the strong feelings of some at that time— including D. L. Moody's son, William—that Speer's views were inconsistent with the founder's wishes.

By all accounts, the young headmaster was a charming and brilliant man, destined for great things. He is usually remembered sitting on a desk or table, his large hands wrapped around one of his knees, talking and laughing with the students. Others recall that often, when they were returning from their parlor dates at Northfield, Speer would be seen driving his beloved dark blue convertible between the campuses, in order to give them a ride back to Mount Hermon. He never called them "boys," as Dr. Cutler, his predecessor, had done. To Speer, Mount Hermon students were always "young men"—a symbolic change, but one very much appreciated by the students.

His brilliance and charisma were matched with a practical, relaxed attitude about day-to-day issues. The maintenance department once complained to him that some of the students walking to class from Crossley Hall were taking a shortcut across the lawn rather than using the paved walk. As a result, the lawn was taking a beating and the students were being disciplined for taking the shortcut. After looking into the matter, Speer gave permission for the boys to walk to class by any route they wished. When a well-defined path appeared, he had it paved. And when a publisher mailed an advertisement to all the students to buy an explicit "marriage manual," Speer announced that he had purchased the book and put it on reserve at the library. "Read it at the library if you want," he told his Mount Hermon men at an assembly, "but don't waste your money buying it."

Elliott Speer resembled the founder not only in his personal warmth and his strong Christian faith, but also in his love of fast driving—although D. L. Moody's vehicles had been horse-drawn. A student at the Northfield Seminary joked in a letter to her boyfriend, "When I think that you may no longer love me, the world becomes a dull murky brown like the walls of [my dormitory], and my conduct becomes reckless as Mr. Speer's driving." Once, on a fund-raising mission while he was president of the schools, he was racing to Springfield to catch the train to New York for a meeting with a group of business executives. Stopped by a policeman for speeding, he explained where he was going and why. The officer let him go, saying, "There'll be no fine, Padre; you'll need all the money you've got and luck too, to raise money in these times."

To many, even some of his friends at Mount Hermon, he was also moving too fast in making changes at the school. He angered many when, at the request of the senior class, he invited Norman Thomas, the leader of the Socialist Party, to speak at the 1934 commencement. William Compton who studied the history of the school has written, apropos of the changes that Speer made:

> It was these changes in rules of behavior that offended traditional alumni and parents more than what happened in the chapel. . . . [O]ne parent . . . refused to allow her daughter to participate in the school-sponsored orchestra because it sometimes performed on Sunday. An outcry also rose over the fact that Bible teachers used a historical rather than a literalist approach. . . . Among conservative faculty members at Mount Hermon, the common gossip was that Speer was lowering standards and listening to students more than faculty. Recollections from that time elicit phrases like hypocritical, sanctimonious, Devil incarnate, blackmail, liar, and crook. . . . And

nothing could more vividly symbolize the community polarization than the murder of Elliott Speer, which must have had its roots in some deeply held hatred. Given the safe assumption that the murder was the act of an unbalanced individual, it is equally reasonable to assume that whoever did it knew the routines of the school well and that the idea for the murder was nurtured on a soil filled with vindictiveness and hate.

Richard Watson, one of the senior members of the Mount Hermon community and a former student at Mount Hermon in the class of 1891, was the superintendent of buildings during Speer's tenure as headmaster. He was also Speer's friend and supporter. He was moved to write to his former classmates when criticism of the headmaster was mounting, "There are a good many things Elliott Speer is doing that I am not in sympathy with and don't believe in, but my knowledge of the man is such that I know he is just as thoroughly interested in the character and Christian education of the boys as ever was D. L. [Moody] or Professor Cutler."

Even after his murder, many said that Elliott Speer had had no enemies. While many disagreed, sometimes vehemently, with the changes he made, his obvious enthusiasm and ability charmed almost all who had personal contact with him.

Why, then, was Elliott Speer murdered? During the investigation, the police publicly speculated on the killer's motives. Was it the act of a religious fanatic, driven to halt Speer's supposed infidelity to Moody's principles? Jealousy on the part of someone who felt himself more deserving of the headmastership? Revenge by a former student expelled from the school or a faculty member who had been dismissed? Or was it the act of a maniac? Why were the authorities, despite massive searches and the questioning of hundreds of people, unable to bring charges against anyone for the murder? And why, when a suspect was identified, were the authorities unwilling or unable to proceed against him?

Elliott Speer

Elliott Speer seems to have been one of those people who go through life with hardly a misstep. He was born into a prominent family. His father, Dr. Robert E. Speer, in addition to being a trustee of the Northfield Schools, had held the top post in the Presbyterian Church: moderator of the General Assembly. At the time of his son's murder, he was senior secretary of the Presbyterian Church's Board of Foreign Missions and a well-known speaker and writer. Elliott Speer's mother had been president of the National Council of the YWCA.

The future headmaster was born on November 1, 1898—All Saints' Day—in Englewood, New Jersey, where he grew up as a quiet and courteous boy. His father, delivering a eulogy to his son at a memorial service in November 1934, told of letters received from old friends who had known Elliott as a boy. These writers described him as full of promise and with "marvelous qualities of mind and character." It is natural, and proper, to discount such testimony given at such a time, but Elliott Speer's remarkable success as an adult provides retrospective support for these observations of his early life.

Dr. Speer recalled in that eulogy the time in 1913 when he and his wife had delivered their son to Phillips Academy at Andover, Massachusetts, where Elliott entered the second-year class. Dr. Speer described the typical parental emotion when "with fear and trembling we saw his little boat put out to sea." Elliott, however, seems to have had little trouble navigating through prep school. His letters to his parents displayed his interests in sports, school pranks, and food from home. He had serious adventures, too: an attack of acute appendicitis and an escape from a burning dormitory by climbing down an ice-covered ladder on a winter night. He was already a religious person who read his Bible regularly. While at Andover, he led a group of fellow students in mission work among the poor children of the mill workers in Lawrence, Massachusetts. This religious bent, no doubt, was less unusual at that time than it is now, but even then it was not the norm for prep school students. Mr. Allan V. Heely, a teacher at Andover, writing after the murder, recalled the young student:

> He seemed to have found the way in which he wished to walk; and he was not afraid to walk at times alone, if that were necessary. Quickness of impulse and a ready tongue sometimes got him into trouble. . . . At Andover Elliott was a busy and useful citizen. Always a ready speaker, he was President of Philo, the old debating club. . . . He helped edit the school paper, and was on the student and athletic councils. Senior year he was President of the Society of Inquiry, the School's religious organization. That was his main concern. His life was set even then along the paths he later followed. Religious interest among schoolboys has not usually been fashionable. Socially it presents certain risks; it is liable to set a man apart. I don't think Elliott ever thought of this. He simply expressed himself naturally.

From Andover, Elliott was accepted at Princeton, where he began his studies in the fall of 1916. Again, he was involved in the religious life of the school, for which he was known as a "Christer" among that very secular student body. Again he was involved with editing the school newspaper, *The Princetonian*. He also was a member of the lightweight crew. His personal traits were as they had always been. His fellow students recalled his good humor, sincerity, and thoughtfulness.

Elliott's time at Princeton coincided with the First World War. As his father said, "The fever of the war time was in the veins of youth in those years and it was hard for boys to hold steady." So his son, in May 1917 (before the United States finally entered the war), sailed for England to help in the work of the British Army YMCA. While working near the front lines in France, he was involved in a near-fatal motorcycle accident. His friend, Dr. Henry Crane, described him after the accident, "in a dugout just back of the lines near Battlemont, his face half-covered with bandages from the wounds of his accident. There he sat alone, by a crude little stove, his face swathed in the bandages so that he was scarcely recognizable, looking forlorn and disconsolate. But his face lit up immediately on my arrival, and to this day I recall with heartening memories the characteristic, quiet heroism of his glorious spirit." By the time he returned from Europe in the summer of 1918, Speer was convinced of the futility of war. Nevertheless, he was attempting to enlist as a naval aviator when the war ended.

Following the devastation of the war, an epidemic of influenza struck both Europe and the United States in 1918. Elliott was living with his parents in Englewood, New Jersey, at that time, and in his eulogy his father recalled his reaction:

> In the influenza epidemic of 1918 when the supply of doctors and nurses was too small and a new temporary hospital had to be improvised, he threw himself in as a helper doing the most menial tasks from washing sheets and nursing the sick to burying the dead, and just turning the balance between hope and despair in many a life. . . . Always afterwards folk of every condition in life would stop him when he was in Englewood to thank him for helping to pull them through.

Elliott's Princeton class, divided by the war service that many had chosen, graduated piecemeal. Elliott received his degree, in theology, in February 1921.

The next month he married Holly, who had graduated from Vassar and was the sister of one of his closest friends. The newlyweds sailed for Scotland later that month, where Elliott began his studies at the Theological College of the United Free Church in Edinburgh. He completed two years' work in three terms and returned to the United States in the spring of 1922. He then joined the staff of the Old First Presbyterian Church in New York City, where he was put in charge of the Bethlehem Chapel in Greenwich Village, in the midst of a largely Italian immigrant community. Although he was in that position for only two years, he impressed his superiors and the people of the community. One of his coworkers described him as "outstanding in understanding, in outlook, in courtesy, in charm."

He then moved to Lafayette College in Pennsylvania, where, in September of 1924, he was appointed chaplain and head of the Bible Department. It was during his first year at Lafayette that he was ordained as a minister by the Presbytery of Jersey City. Dr. John MacCracken, the president of the college, wrote that the youthful minister had an impact on the Lafayette students:

> From the day that the college heard that deep voice of his fill the college chapel without hesitation or tremor, it recognized him as a valiant man, sincere, unafraid, teaching with the authority which belongs to one whose doctrine is also his life. . . . He was entirely free of self-consciousness. He belonged to an automobile age, accustomed to move forward quickly and certainly with little expectation or thought of obstacles. . . . He won everyone's confidence and cooperation and affection. . . . The reaction of the students was described by one sophomore in his diary, "He's a prince." "He's a prince" was the unanimous verdict of the student body. . . . Elliott Speer's mind was open and constructive and reverent.

Elliott's connection with the Northfield Schools began in 1926, when he joined his father on the board of trustees. The following year, the board elected him president of the schools, replacing William Moody, one of D. L.'s sons, who was ill. Mr. Moody was named chairman. The trustees apparently thought that Moody would act as an advisor or mentor to the young president. Moody, however, seems to have assumed that Speer would assist him. Unfortunately, this misunderstanding resulted two years later in Moody's noisy resignation. The *New York Times* of February 11, 1929, gave the story front-page coverage, its headline: "Moody Quits in Row over His Leadership of Bible Schools."

This dispute placed Robert Speer in an uncomfortable position between the prickly and conservative Moody, of whom he was very fond, and Elliott. Nevertheless, he rejected Moody's charge that Elliott's views were in conflict with the ideals of the founder, and he voted with the other trustees to accept Moody's resignation, saying that the school administration was "doing its best to preserve those ideals [of D. L. Moody] under the changed conditions of the days in which we live." The unanimous vote of the trustees confirmed what the election of Elliott Speer as their president had already shown: that they were determined to modernize the schools, even at the risk of alienating the more conservative alumni and faculty.

The youthful Speer's first task as president of the Northfield Schools was to cure their financial woes. The schools had incurred an operating deficit of over $100,000 in 1928. Speer responded to this short-term emergency by sending out 250,000 letters appealing to the public. The money was secured, but he recognized that this method of financing the schools' operations was expensive, time-consuming, and uncertain. After conferring with experts in fund-raising and investigating the financial needs of the schools, Speer recommended a $3 million fund drive to provide pensions for the faculty, repairs to the buildings, and an endowment fund that would yield a predictable income. The launching of this campaign took place amid general enthusiasm and a stock market boom in September 1929. The timing, though, was less than propitious. One month later the stock market crash marked the end of the prosperous Roaring Twenties and the beginning of the Great Depression.

In October 1929, the stock market began a sickening slide, a symptom of serious problems afflicting the country's—and the world's—economy. The *New York Times* average of fifty leading stocks lost nearly half its value between September 3 and November 13. In 1930, 1,345 banks failed. Unemployment, slightly over 3 percent in 1929, reached nearly 25 percent three years later. Five million people were unemployed by 1930; 13 million by the end of 1933. The belief in the inevitability of economic growth—a characteristic of the 1920s—collapsed with the economy. Belt tightening became the new fashion.

In the face of the stock market crash, some at the schools recommended delaying the fund-raising campaign, but Elliott Speer was not to be discouraged. By the middle of 1931, he and his colleagues had raised $2.75 million dollars, a nearly miraculous accomplishment in the circumstances.

At the same time, the schools had been searching for a new principal for the Northfield Seminary. Elliott Speer found someone much like himself to take the job. Mira Wilson, who was to become his good friend as well as coworker, was a professor of religion and biblical literature at Smith College. She had received her bachelor's degree in divinity at Boston University in 1917. She was only a few years older than Elliott, and she shared his optimism that the schools could update and improve their academic and social standards without losing their essentially religious nature. Annie Mildred Herring, a member of the Northfield staff, who knew both Wilson and Speer said, "These two were of the same cut—intelligent, humane, attractive, and both from backgrounds of refinement and scholarship. . . . They were eager to create an atmosphere for the boys and girls in the Schools where the spirit could be nurtured and made free along with the development of the mind." Mira Wilson became principal of the Northfield Seminary in the fall of 1929.

At this time the headmaster of Mount Hermon was sixty-seven-year-old Henry Cutler, who had taken the job in 1890. After forty years as headmaster he was planning to retire, so a search for someone to run Mount Hermon was imminent. At the same time, Elliott Speer had concluded that the office of president of the board of trustees should become a part-time, nonsalaried job. When Cutler learned, probably from Elliott, that the young president would prefer working directly with students to raising money or being an administrator, Cutler enthusiastically recommended him as his successor. The board of trustees readily agreed. In spite of the fact that the two men were very different—the dour Cutler was short, compact, strict, and the product of an earlier age, whereas Elliott Speer was tall, slim, fun-loving, and thoroughly modern—they had become friends. The announcement of Speer's appointment was deeply disappointing to the conservatives on the faculty and among the alumni, including at least one person, Dean Elder, who had expected to succeed Cutler.

This trustees' decision was announced in 1931. But the trustees decided to allow Elliott and his family time, before assuming the duties of headmaster, to return to Edinburgh for another year of study, during which he worked on his thesis: "The Influence on the Formation of Character of Certain Religious Doctrines—a Pedagogical Estimate." During that year, he also visited a number of English "public" (that is, private) schools to learn all he could to prepare himself for his new position. (He had spent a considerable amount of time in Scotland and had made many friends there. After his murder, a leading Scottish newspaper wrote, "He was a man of great personal charm as well as boundless vitality, and his tragic death will be mourned by a large circle of friends in this country.")

The social changes that Elliott Speer initiated at Mount Hermon after assuming the headmaster's position, such as allowing dancing and interscholastic athletics, permitting the students to read the newspapers on Sunday (afternoon), and the like, do not seem revolutionary looking back seventy years. Surely, they just brought the school into the twentieth century. After all, in 1934 the sex symbol Mae West was one of Hollywood's most popular actresses, and Cecil B. DeMille's sensual *Cleopatra* was drawing enthusiastic crowds to the movies. But, as we have seen, Speer's liberalizing at Mount Hermon sparked controversy on the part of some very conservative alumni and members of the administration, who felt that Speer was being unfaithful to the founder's vision.

There is no question, though, that Elliott Speer was deeply interested in educating young people, and he had that rare ability both to impress his elders—such as the trustees of the school—and to inspire affection and respect in young people.

One of Elliott's best friends at Mount Hermon was David

Birdsall—the first person, other than the doctor, to be called after Elliott was shot. His son, Richard, who was four when he first encountered Speer in 1928, recalled that when both his family and the Speers lived in East Northfield (before they moved to the Mount Hermon campus), he was often asked to run over to Morgan's Garage to get a pack of Camel cigarettes (for fifteen cents) for Mr. Speer. "It was a great honor; I would do anything for that man. . . . Somehow life became more dramatic, more of an adventure during Mr. Speer's visits. He radiated energy and beyond that grace; in his presence you lived on a higher level than you had thought possible."

Like many who remembered Elliott Speer, Richard Birdsall recalled his love of cars and speed. Richard's parents told him of returning from a concert at Northampton in the middle of winter with Speer at the wheel of his convertible: "Mr. Speer remarked on the sparkling effect of the new snow as it reflected the light of the full moon and then suggested that since they were all warmly dressed they should try riding with the top down." They completed the trip in the updated "one horse open sleigh."

From a young age, Elliott Speer had a deep religious faith. As to the education of young people, though, he was still struggling to develop his ideas. As the title of his thesis, "The Influence on the Formation of Character of Certain Religious Doctrines—a Pedagogical Estimate," suggests, he believed that religion and education should function together to form students of good character. Although he was not certain how this could best be accomplished, Elliott Speer was sure that the early teen years—the secondary school years—were crucial in character development. When Richard Watson, one of the oldest members of the Mount Hermon community, worried aloud that Speer would leave the school to run a college, the headmaster reassured him, "I would rather be headmaster of a preparatory school than president of a college because [this is] . . . the formative period of a boy's life." This was, as Speer probably knew, almost an exact quotation from D. L. Moody.

While thinking about the problems of secondary education during his stay in Scotland, Elliott wrote his brother-in-law:

I think my point of view is something like this. In the past some of the great religious ideas have exerted a tremendous and beneficial influence in enlarging men's lives (isn't that what we mean by forming character). They are not doing that today. I believe it is not because they are untrue, but because they are not understood. Can they be restated for modern understanding (which means, doesn't it, in terms that fit modern experience), and if so, will they then influence character, develop personality, enlarge life, in fact save men? That is my problem.

On another occasion, he prayed, "We want to help working children to the opportunity to live. We don't know how. We want to help on world brotherhood and put an end to race hatred, but we don't know how. We want to help stop war, but we don't know how. We want to help, so let us learn in order that we may truly serve, and that, in Christ's name, His Will may be done."

Elliott Speer showed that deep religious conviction could be combined with a lively, curious intellect and a love of life and adventure. On his bookshelves he had books on such serious contemporary subjects as economics and sociology, but he also enjoyed mystery novels. He was never sanctimonious, and he had a gift for memorable gestures. Former student William Cole recalled Elliott Speer speaking at an assembly about obsolete customs. He compared these to the buttons on jacket sleeves, which were sewn on originally for a reason most had forgotten: to prevent soldiers from wiping their noses on their uniform sleeves. Thus he told the students that today buttons on jacket sleeves were obsolete—unless, he said, your jacket was made in London. At that point, he unbuttoned the sleeves of his jacket and rolled them up. The students remembered his lessons.

He loved being headmaster. In September 1933, a year after starting the job, he wrote to Wilfred Fry, who had succeeded him as president of the board of trustees:

I cannot recall a busier week since I came to Northfield than the one which is just closing. The influx of students swamped us; the class sections have been too big; we have not had enough dormitory room; we have had to get an extra teacher; in fact, we have practically had to rearrange the schedule of classes and the curriculum during the last few days. *It is the sort of work in which one delights,* and I am sorry that it has made a delay in answering your letter. (emphasis added)

Another reminiscence from one of the students who came under Elliott Speer's spell illustrates the relationship that he developed with his "young men." The headmaster had begun loosening some of the school's restrictive rules, and the students, naturally, were looking forward to more liberalizing:

> With such an understanding man at the helm we students naturally felt that some of the very strict rules at school might be relaxed. Some were. However, this man was no ticket to making Mt. Hermon a country club life. It seemed that we had to go to chapel every day and twice on Sunday. We did have optional chapel on Wednesday because that was a prayer meeting, and for some reason it had been decided by those who made such decisions, that it was not exactly right to make a prayer meeting compulsory. On the first Thursday, after Mr. Speer's first Wednesday [chapel service], he announced in chapel that in the future chapel would be compulsory on Wednesday. He had attended chapel the day before and he had been shocked to find only 10 or 12 boys out of 500 attended the service.
>
> Now, until this point, in the fifty years of Mount Hermon's existence, any pronouncement from the mouth of the headmaster was absolute law. His position might be likened unto that of Moses descending from Mt. Sinai with his tablets containing the Ten Commandments. The student body did something that it had never done before. The boys booed. They booed louder and louder. The august members of the faculty frowned. They seemed to be trying to spot from their seats on the platform just who among the students might be called the ringleaders of this unheard-of performance. Mr. Speer smiled as the boys booed. He turned and looked at the faculty members on the platform, and his smile turned into a large grin. He looked back out over the student body and he laughed. The booing continued; in fact, it became louder. The louder we booed, the funnier he seemed to think that the whole matter was.

Then it happened. I have never been in a situation to ever see such a thing happen. From nowhere, from everywhere, in the chapel the booing was being drowned out. Actually, the change of sounds might be compared to a huge organ as the notes change suddenly, yet confidently, from one tune to another. . . . The booing was being drowned out by—applause. It was almost a spooky, hair-raising feeling to sense the booing sound drift off, and a sound of clapping take over. Within ten or fifteen seconds there was not a boo to be heard, just a solid student body of five hundred boys applauding the man who had the courage, and the decency, and the understanding to take our booing, and know it for what it was. No malice was in his heart or mind. No thought of punishment for our action crossed his mind. Our applause was for a man who could stand alone, give us an order that we did not want, take our reply without pulling any rank on his part—and laugh at us. We all felt that he laughed at the faculty on the platform, too. He knew that he was the boss. He proved it to us by his laughter, not by his new order that we attend chapel on Wednesdays in the future. No man ever has had the love and respect that Elliott Speer had from that day on from his boys. We did in truth worship that man.

The story had a short p.s. on it. The next week, Mr. Speer announced in chapel that the senior class president, Tom Kay, had informed him that a great hardship had come to pass because of the compulsory chapel on Wednesday. It seems that Tom had told him that many boys used the time . . . from 12:00 to 12:20 to write home to their mothers. He told us that he did not mean to cause such a hardship to be worked on the relationship between such good boys and their mothers. Therefore, he would rescind the new chapel order for all the boys who wrote home to mother at that time. This was greeted with much cheering and applause. Then he asked for a show of hands of all the boys who wrote home to mother at that hour of the week. Every boy in chapel raised his hand.

"I am so glad to see that all of you write home to your mothers each week. All of you who raised your hands will be excused from Wednesday chapel." More cheering. We felt that we had fooled him after all.

Elliott Speer doffs his cap to the graduating class of 1934.
Courtesy of Edwin Thompson.

"Oh, one more thing [Mr. Speer continued]. Just to keep this new ruling running right I want one thing in exchange. I want each of the boys who raised his hand to come to my office with his schedule, and I will try to find twenty minutes somewhere else in your busy week when you can write home to mother." This was greeted by the loudest laughter that has ever been heard in the Mount Hermon chapel. Every boy knew that he had all Sunday afternoon free, and all day Monday free.

Five hundred boys attended Wednesday prayer meetings at Mount Hermon from that day forward. It was twenty minutes a week that we spent in salute to the man.

Elliott's father, in his eulogy, quoted from some of Elliott's papers and sermons. In one of them Elliott had written: "Christ never used any methods, never did things the same way twice. As for our books of method I am convinced that every man formulated his method afterwards, not before. Who would rely on a book of instructions in making love? Avoid some one else's formula." Dr. Speer ended his eulogy for his son tearfully. "God rest his dear and radiant soul."

The Police Investigation

Friday Night and Saturday

A Mystery Novel and Some Scraps

The investigators charged with finding the murderer faced a dauntingly difficult case. The crime scene included a 1,200-acre wooded campus, bordered by the wide, muddy Connecticut River, in a sparsely populated rural area—a nearly infinite number of places for the murderer and his weapon to be hidden. The killer had left no footprints on the hard surface outside the headmaster's window, and precious few other clues. The victim, as headmaster and a prominent member of the community, had close contact with hundreds of students and alumni and a large faculty and administration, any of whom might have real or imagined reasons for wanting him removed. Complicating matters, the investigators would have to rely upon many of these potential suspects for information. Finally, the public spotlight on the crime was bound to—and did—attract large numbers of rumors and "tips" from members of the public, well-meaning or otherwise.

The investigators arrived. They included Lieutenant Albert Dasey, who was a State Police detective from Greenfield (the county seat, about ten miles south of Mount Hermon), and some troopers from the Shelburne Falls barracks. At about the same time the district attorney, Joseph T. Bartlett, also from Greenfield, appeared and took charge of the scene. Dasey, short and swarthy, with his dark hair brushed back, was an experienced detective. Bartlett was earnest, slim and lanky, and wore wire-rimmed glasses. Although it was too dark to conduct an effective search outside, it was a simple matter for Bartlett and Dasey to conclude that the killer had fired a shotgun from a few yards outside the headmaster's study window. The shattered window, the torn curtain, the holes in the study walls, and the trail of blood from the headmaster's desk to the hall testified to the murderer's method, and its effect.

The troopers began a search of Ford Cottage for clues, while Bartlett and Dasey questioned the occupants. The troopers soon found a .22-caliber target pistol in Speer's desk, prompting them to speculate that he had felt the need to protect himself from enemies. Bartlett and Dasey learned, while questioning those who had been in the house at the time of the shooting, that no one had heard either of the Speers' two dogs bark before the shot was heard. This clue naturally raised in their minds the possibility that the killer was well known to the dogs and, therefore, to the family. (Those familiar with Sherlock Holmes will recall the nonbarking dog incident in the story "Silver Blaze." Inspector Gregory asks Holmes, "Is there any point to which you would wish to draw my attention?" Holmes says, "To the curious incident of the dog in the night-time." The inspector replies, "The dog did nothing in the night-time." "That was the curious incident," answers Holmes.) On further investigation, though, it turned out that the dogs' silence proved nothing. The puppy, Amy, had been locked in a kennel away from the front of the house at the time of the shooting, and Andy, the Speers' huge black Newfoundland, was an affable campus pet, not the watchdog type.

Another find by an alert trooper, however, remains one of the most intriguing and tantalizing aspects of this story. Among the books in Speer's library, the trooper found a mystery novel, *The Public School Murder*, by the English writer R. C. Woodthorpe, that describes the murder of the headmaster of an English private (what the English call "public") school. The trooper must have been astonished when he read this account of the fictional murder: "There . . . at that window . . . the headmaster sat writing. . . . The light shone upon him; he was a conspicuous target. . . . [T]he murderer crept stealthily along the edge of the grass until he was within a yard or two. One shot was enough." Further on in the book, the chairman of the board of governors of the school, a businessman playing detective, reconstructs the crime, calling the hypothetical killer "Jones":

> I imagine Jones acted for the next few minutes in utterly cold-blooded fashion. He was in an exalted mood. He felt himself the instrument of—Oh, very well, . . . we will say he was possessed of a devil. He went very calmly to carry out his purpose. His step was firm. His hand was perfectly steady. Under cover of the night he slipped into the quadrangle. He walked on the grass. . . . He came within two or three yards of the headmaster's window. Thorold [the headmaster] was writing. He was quite unconscious of the man who stood so close. He did not look up. This man—Jones, we are calling him—had already loaded the rifle with one of his two cartridges. Jones, at point-blank range, raised the rifle to his shoulder. He took deliberate aim. He fired. Then he hastily ejected the cartridge, remembering to put the empty case in his pocket, and loaded again. But a second shot was not necessary.

In the novel, the murder weapon was found in a nearby lake. Shadow Lake on the Mount Hermon campus lies between Ford Cottage and the main road—one of the escape routes available to the murderer. Not only did this mystery novel seem to hint at a place to search for the murder weapon; it was learned that Speer had regularly loaned his books to several Mount Hermon faculty members. Had the murderer been one of the readers? And had Woodthorpe's novel suggested the method the killer used to kill Mount Hermon's headmaster?

At about 2:00 A.M., Bartlett decided to question the thirty-five "old boys" who had returned to campus early, all of whom were sleeping in Crossley Hall across the campus. Stunned with sleep and shaken by the news brought by the police, the boys were interrogated. Almost all of them had been attending a meeting in Crossley when the murder had occurred. When the questioning was finished, there was nothing more to be done until light allowed a search of the area around Ford Cottage.

Soon, of course, the press arrived. The murder was to be front-page news around the country. Bartlett, from the beginning, was open to a surprising degree with the reporters. He frankly admitted that he and the police had no real clues to the killer's identity. "Anybody's guess in this murder is as good as mine." Nevertheless, his experiences overnight on campus had convinced him of one thing: the murderer must have been "a person very familiar with the terrain of the school. In the utter blackness which prevails on the campus at night no stranger could have found his way to the house in its remote location and then escaped."

Anyone visiting the school, even today, would likely agree with Bartlett. The roads onto the Mount Hermon campus wound through woods and past farms and other isolated houses belonging to faculty and administrative employees of the school. None led directly to the headmaster's house. Nor were there any signs pointing to Ford Cottage. Once on the main part of the campus, with its dormitories and classroom buildings on the lower level and more dormitories, including the large Crossley Hall, the dining hall, and Memorial Chapel, on the higher level, Ford Cottage would not be obvious. It stands on a high point, but it is hidden behind the chapel and backed by woods. Bartlett was right; the house is isolated and remote. Certainly the killer had to have been someone familiar with the campus.

As soon as it was light on Saturday morning, the police, helped by the students and others, began a systematic search of the grounds around Ford Cottage. But it was not until the afternoon that two bits of shotgun wadding and a piece of cardboard from a shotgun shell were found. It had been breezy on the night of the shooting, and these light pieces of evidence must have blown away from the spot where the killer had stood. Captain Charles Van Amburgh, a firearms expert, deduced from these meager clues that the murder weapon was a 12-gauge shotgun loaded with double-o buckshot. From the pattern of holes in the window screen of the headmaster's study, Van Amburgh further concluded that the shotgun had been fitted with a "choke" muzzle, which focuses the shot into a narrow area, increasing its killing power. Van Amburgh also determined that the shot had been fired from a distance of about 30 feet from the headmaster's window. The killer, he said, had stood by a small maple tree, perhaps steadying the gun on one of its branches.

Armed with a description of the type of gun that had been used, the police began checking on those who owned shotguns on campus and contacting nearby sporting goods stores to identify recent purchasers of shotguns and ammunition. Although several people living on campus acknowledged owning shotguns and delivered them to the police, none of these guns was regarded as a possible murder weapon—some were not 12-gauge, and none had been fired recently.

In the course of questioning the students, faculty, and others connected to the school, the police heard rumors and speculation, all of which they had to investigate. One story was that a former student had been in town a few weeks before and had confided to a local boy that he had a list of "Twenty-one Punishments" of which he had already accomplished seven. "The next one," he had said, according to the rumor, "means I'm going to get Speer." The press learned of this rumor, probably from Bartlett, and eagerly reported the melodramatic tale to the public. The police soon found the young man who was the subject of the story at his college, Washington and Lee in Lexington, Virginia. He had had a brilliant record at Mount Hermon and was a respected student leader at college. Moreover, he had an airtight alibi for the night of the shooting. The next day, the police assured the reporters that the rumor was wholly unfounded. The records do not disclose the source of the rumor or what, if any, action was taken against those who started it.

Although this story of an angry ex-student proved to be base-less, the authorities did begin compiling lists of students who had been expelled and of faculty and administrative personnel who had been dismissed.

Another informant called the police to say he could describe the killer. Upon questioning, it turned out that this gentleman had given a stranger a ride on the day before the killing, and the man had said he was going to Mount Hermon. There was nothing more.

The investigators (and the press) heard stories of bitter fac-tional disagreements within the school's administration and fac-ulty over Speer's liberalizing policies. As mentioned, in addition to allowing the Mount Hermon boys to have social contacts with girls from the Northfield Seminary and to participate in interscholastic athletics, Speer had also invited the socialist Norman Thomas to speak at the school the previous June. According to some, the more conservative members of the faculty and staff felt very strongly that Speer was leading the school away from its strongly Christian tradition, and the appearance of the politically radical Thomas on campus may have been the last straw. The press sug-gested that the murder might have been motivated by what they came to call "Fundamentalism." The *New York Times* attributed to "investigators" the assertion that "there is a possibility that one of Dr. Speer's opponents, maddened over the prospect of the opening of another term Monday under what he regarded as an unfit leader, might have goaded himself into the shooting."

At the end of the first day, it was becoming apparent to Bart-lett and the police that this investigation could prove to be a long one. They had started down all the obvious paths looking for sus-pects with motives, but had little to show for it. Indeed, the only physical evidence was the wadding, the small pieces of a shotgun shell, the shattered window, and the shotgun slugs. They had ru-mors and vague stories of possible motives, including a religious motive, but no murder weapon and no eyewitnesses. And they had a large wooded campus to search, with hundreds of students scheduled to arrive on the scene in the following week.

Sunday

∽

The Memorial Service and a Committee

Bartlett briefed the press, admitting, "We are up against a stone wall." He said that on Monday the search for the murder weapon would intensify. Evidently feeling that Shadow Lake was a likely place to find the murder weapon (a suspicion perhaps suggested by *The Public School Murder*), Bartlett reported that the lake would be drained. The investigators also planned to begin a thorough search of the woods on campus and decided to employ a diver to search the Connecticut River near the bridge that crosses the river between Mount Hermon and Northfield. The police theorized that the killer might have driven from the scene and thrown the gun off the bridge.

This latter plan, to search the river near the bridge, was certainly the result of what the police had learned from witnesses about a car at the scene of the shooting. Speer's maid, Florence George, told them that she had heard a car drive off after she had heard the shot. The Bodleys and Dierigs, who had been talking outside the Mount Hermon post office before the shooting, told the police that they had seen a car, possibly a Franklin sedan, headed toward the headmaster's house. After they heard the sound of a shot, they said, the car passed by them again and drove off rapidly in the direction of Northfield.

While the investigators planned their next steps, the school's administration quickly made plans to keep the school operating smoothly in spite of the killing. About five hundred students would be arriving for the fall term in the next two days. By Sunday, eight out of the seventeen trustees had arrived in response to Dean Elder's calls and telegrams, and they attended a meeting at the rambling Northfield Inn, a few miles from campus.

The president of the board was Wilfred Washington Fry. The son of a minister, he had attended Mount Hermon from 1892 to 1896, after which he went to work for the YMCA. In 1904, he married the daughter of the owner of N. W. Ayer & Son, a large and successful Philadelphia advertising agency. Five years later his father-in-law finally persuaded Fry to leave his work for the YMCA to come to work at Ayer, and by the late 1920s he was president of the firm. Fry was a man of strong principles. He had refused to produce advertising for alcoholic beverages after Prohibition had been repealed. He said that accepting liquor advertising business would put the agency "in the position of making alcohol attractive to the youth of this country," which, he added, would be "for us, an impossible situation."

The first order of business for the trustees who had assembled at the Northfield Inn was to decide who would shoulder the head-master's duties at Mount Hermon. After considerable discussion, Fry and the other trustees decided to appoint a committee of three to act until a new headmaster was named. They selected David R. Porter, the new head of the Bible Department, as chairman of the committee, with Professor Nelson A. Jackson, head of the Mathe-matics Department, and Dean Elder as the two other members. Porter was starting his first year teaching at Mount Hermon. He was a graduate of Bowdoin College in Maine and a Rhodes scholar. He was unprepossessing in appearance, with round glasses, a long face, and a long, straight nose. He was quiet, even shy. The students came to call him "Jesus" Porter since his appear-ance and quiet manner suggested puritanical piety. They would have been surprised to learn that Porter had been on the Bowdoin football team and, in a game against Harvard, had returned a Har-vard fumble 100 yards for a touchdown. After the play, he was asked, "Why didn't you fall on the ball, Dave?" He answered, "I thought that I might do better." (Ironically, he later wrote an arti-cle in the *Educational Review* entitled "Football: An Impossible Intercollegiate Sport," advocating that it be replaced by intramural rugby.)

Professor Jackson, rather self-effacing but dedicated to the teaching of mathematics, was a graduate of Bates College in Maine and had a master's degree from Columbia University. He was also the author of numerous articles about teaching methods and an algebra textbook. On the standard form that Mount Her-mon used to keep information on the faculty, "Information for the Northfield Schools' Who's Who," there is a space in which the

Wilfred Fry, president of the board of trustees and amateur sleuth. He recognized the crucial clue.
Courtesy of N. W. Ayer archives.

faculty member is asked to "add any interesting items not covered by the questions above." Professor Jackson had typed in: "So far as I know there is nothing interesting about myself."

Elder was fifty-five years old, but he looked older. He had been a student at Mount Hermon, then a proctor, then head of the school's Agriculture Department. When the Agriculture Department was abolished, Dr. Cutler named Elder dean. He was considered an authority on the breeding of Holstein cattle, and under his direction the Mount Hermon herd had become one of the best in the East. (When he died, an obituary in a dairy trade association magazine lamented, "In [Elder's] passing, the Holstein cow loses one of her most stalwart advocates.") Although the trustees knew that Elder felt that he was capable of taking on the headmaster's duties, and badly wanted the position, they also knew that educationally, and for other reasons, he was not an appropriate choice to succeed Speer.

The fact that Mount Hermon owned a herd of cattle will be surprising to those whose image of a prep school is more likely to include world-weary young men with blazers and school ties than young workers milking cows and mucking out the dairy barn before dawn. The fact that the school's dean was known as a cattle expert demonstrates that Mount Hermon was true to the ideas of D. L. Moody. The world-famous evangelist had believed in the dignity of physical labor as well as the value of education. His schools reflected those beliefs—all the students had to work ten hours a week. Freshmen could find themselves in the stifling laundry, or shoveling snow in the bitter New England winters, or, yes, milking Dean Elder's prized Holsteins. By senior year, students typically had more responsible jobs—supervising work groups, editing *The Hermonite* (the school paper), or working in the relative comfort of the library. But all had to work as well as attend chapel at least four times a week and carry a full college preparatory academic schedule.

Elliott Speer had begun liberalizing some aspects of the school and improving its academics, but he had not eliminated the work program—one of the traditions that differentiated the school from its more upper-crust competitors. He also maintained the unique historical characteristic of the school: the practice of admitting only needy students. In April, he had written to a minister who had complained that the school was becoming too exclusive, "In the first place, children of more well-to-do homes are not readily accepted. Our rule today is as it has ever been here at Mount Hermon, that we will not accept those who can afford more expensive schools."

On Sunday, while the investigators continued their search for the killer, a memorial service was held for the murdered headmaster at Ford Cottage. Before a very large number of mourners, the school's chaplain, Rev. Lester P. White, opened the service with Romans, chapter 8, verses 1–14, the first portion of which reads:

> There is therefore now no condemnation to them which are in Christ Jesus, who walk not after the flesh, but after the Spirit. For the law of the Spirit of life in Christ Jesus hath made me free from the law of sin and death. For what the law could not do, in that it was weak through the flesh, God sending his own son in the likeness of sinful flesh, and for sin, condemned sin in the flesh: That the righteousness of the law might be fulfilled in us, who walk not after the flesh, but after the Spirit. For they that are after the flesh do mind the things of the flesh; but they that are after the Spirit the things of the Spirit.

He also read Elliott's favorite hymn, "This Is My Father's World," part of which caught the mood:

> *This is my Father's world:*
> *Oh, let me ne'er forget*
> *That tho' the wrong seems oft so strong,*
> *God is the ruler yet.*

After the service, some of the trustees spoke to the reporters and criticized their newspapers' coverage of the investigation, particularly the focus on "problem boys" who might have had a grudge against the headmaster and the reports of "bitterness" concerning Speer's changes at the school. An unidentified trustee said, "There was feeling. There were those who loved the old ways, but that has all passed." He continued, responding to some stories that the

"Fundamentalists" at the school opposed Speer on the grounds that he was not true to the legacy of D. L. Moody, "The term 'Fundamentalist' as it is generally understood, could not be applied to Dwight L. Moody. His was a religion of joy and hope, not the literal interpretation of hell and eternal damnation."

So the day ended, as the school prepared for the arrival of the students for the fall term, amid the continuing police presence on the campus.

Monday

Investigators Added; New Students Arrive

In the morning new investigative horsepower was added. Brigadier General Daniel Needham, head of the Massachusetts State Police, arrived and took personal charge of the investigation. With him came two detectives, including his highly respected and experienced detective lieutenant, John Stokes. Stokes had added to his reputation earlier in the year by helping to solve the Millen case involving four murders and five robberies by two brothers in eastern Massachusetts. Joining the group who had begun the investigation Friday night, Needham and his detectives began detailed questioning of everyone who was on or near campus on Friday night or who was directly connected to the school. They moved their campus headquarters to Ford Cottage, Holly and her three daughters having left the campus for the relative peace of the New York City home of her parents. The Speer servants, however, remained on campus. According to the papers, their questioning by Bartlett and the police lasted the entire afternoon.

Needham and one of his aides met with Dean Elder and Richard Watson, the superintendent of the school grounds and buildings, who furnished them with a detailed map of all buildings on the campus. Watson was also working on the plan to drain Shadow Lake.

At the same time, 249 "new boys"—students attending Mount Hermon for the first time—arrived and had to be welcomed, registered, fed, and installed in their dormitories. The 35 "old boys" already on campus acted as their guides, helping the new students begin the adjustment to their new lives. No doubt the Mount Hermon faculty and administration also had to reassure them, and especially their parents, that the school was safe and would function normally despite the presence of large numbers of police and the press.

The welcoming edition of the school paper, *The Hermonite,* printed a letter from Speer on its first page: "Greetings and Welcome! From 500 homes and for 5,000 reasons, Hermon men will be arriving on the Hill to start the new year. During your days here, we hope Hermon will be a home to you. But above all, we hope that during the work and play you will, in the words of Theodore Roosevelt in his advice to American boys, constantly 'hit the line hard.'" Elliott Speer's picture was framed in black.

Tuesday

∽

The Search for the Murder Weapon and Suspects Continues

This was the day most of the "old boys" were scheduled to arrive. As they made their way up the main road to the campus, they could see Carroll Rikert, who normally worked at the school farm, dragging Shadow Lake in an effort to find the still-missing shotgun (and thereby to avoid draining the lake). No doubt they were wondering whether the annual rope-pull tug of war across the lake between the senior and junior classes would be canceled.

Also arriving on this day was Edwin P. "Red" Thompson of Westerly, Rhode Island, of the class of 1934, who had been the president of the Senior Council for the previous school year. Bartlett had asked Thompson to meet with Dean Elder and to select possible suspects from a list of students who had been expelled during Speer's regime. So, before beginning his college studies at Princeton, Thompson returned to Mount Hermon. According to Bartlett, Thompson and Elder selected the names of six students who had been expelled. Bartlett said his investigators would check on the whereabouts of those students at the time of the murder.

Thompson, though, was strongly of the opinion that this would be another dead end. He said, "I have heard boys say, after they had been fired [expelled], that they would rather be disciplined by Dr. [sic] Speer than by any man in the world. They knew they always had an even break. He never did a mean or unfair thing in his life."

In the morning, since classes had not yet started, the police employed one hundred students, divided into squads of ten, each led by a state trooper, to continue the search for the shotgun. They searched in the woods and hunted step by step over hundreds of acres along the campus roads for the murder weapon, in vain. The same prize also eluded Fred Wallace, an expert diver from Somerville, Massachusetts, who arrived to begin the search of the Connecticut River bottom near the bridge between Mount Hermon and Northfield. He spent several hours diving in an area extending 100 yards south (downstream) from the bridge.

The Reverend R. M. Russell, who had officiated on Monday at the headmaster's funeral in Larchmont, New York, also met at length with the police. For once, the content of the interview was not shared with the press. However, the New York Times reported that Russell had cleared up several details concerning individuals who were acquaintances or associates of Speer.

Two questions that the investigators had posed and that had been repeated in the press were answered. First, the police reported that they were satisfied that the fact that the Speers' dogs had not barked did not constitute a clue that the murderer was well known to either the dogs or the family. Andy, the big Newfoundland, had growled vaguely at one of the policemen, but had clearly little interest in strangers. The puppy, as already noted, was in a kennel behind Ford Cottage at the time of the shooting.

On the issue of the pistol found in Speer's desk, his friend David Birdsall explained that he had purchased it several years before for the headmaster. At the time, Birdsall had been a cashier of the Northfield Bank, of which Speer was a director. Birdsall was buying pistols for the security agents at the bank, and Speer asked him to buy a target pistol for him. According to Birdsall (by this time the purchasing agent for the school), Speer had rarely used it and never carried it with him. The police and press speculation that the pistol showed that Speer felt threatened by an enemy did not impress Birdsall, who had become almost a member of the Speer family. "Elliott had no enemies," he said.

Albert Roberts, the executive secretary of the board of trustees, made two announcements. First, he said that letters of condolence were arriving at the rate of three hundred a day. Second, he announced that the trustees had agreed that if the district and state authorities were unable to solve the killing, the alumni and the school would take a hand by hiring private investigators. Although Roberts did not know this, Wilfred Fry, the president of the board, had already been considering this step. Doubts about a member of the Mount Hermon community were beginning to form in Fry's mind. He had not yet shared these suspicions with the police or even with the other trustees.

Wednesday

∽

General Fear and More Dead Ends

The day began with a telephone call to investigation headquarters claiming that the superintendent of schools of nearby Shelburne Falls had been shot at while driving along the Mohawk Trail highway, some twenty-four miles from Mount Hermon. This, naturally, generated excitement and even hope among the investigators: was there a serial killer preying on New England educators? Upon investigation, however, this turned into yet another time-consuming false alarm. The superintendent thought he had heard a shot while he was driving, not a rare event in rural areas at that time. Sometime later he stopped his car and noticed pockmarks on it. Influenced by the local anxiety about the Speer shooting, he concluded that someone had shot at him with a shotgun. The police, though, after examining his car, concluded that the marks had been caused by loose gravel on the road. They interviewed a number of people who lived near the point of the alleged shooting, none of whom had heard any shots. This incident demonstrated the nervousness, even panic, that affected the area while the search for the killer continued fruitlessly. The *New York Times* of September 20 reported: "The fear is general, almost approaching a belief, that somewhere in the hill communities of Northern Massachusetts, a fanatic or a murderer with a shotgun is at large and that it is possible that he may have other figures marked for slaughter."

There did seem to be some reasons for optimism that a break in the case might be near when a clerk in a Greenfield gun store recalled selling four shotgun shells to someone shortly before the shooting. Police said that photographs of several people connected to the school would be shown to the clerk in hopes of finally identifying the killer. Also, the investigators turned up several letters from the school files that, they said, contained significant information about events leading to the murder. The letters, according to the police, had been mailed from Syracuse and Utica, New York, but they refused to give any more details. This information, however, led nowhere.

A number of earlier leads had already proved to be dead ends. The draining of Shadow Lake was completed and no gun was found. Fred Wallace, the diver, completed his search of the Connecticut River near the bridge. He had turned up two rusty bicycle frames and an old sewing machine, but no shotgun. (The failure to find the gun does not mean that it was not there, as the police later proved by throwing objects into the river from the bridge. Divers, even knowing exactly where the objects entered the river, could not find them.) One other gun did appear when the school blacksmith, Daniel Van Valkenburgh, delivered his shotgun to the police. It was a 20-gauge weapon, smaller than that which had been used to kill Speer. That, and Van Valkenburgh's satisfactory accounting for his activities on September 14, persuaded the police that he was not a suspect. In addition, Lieutenant Dasey told the press that they had checked on the whereabouts of a former insane asylum inmate who might have had a grudge against Speer. They found, however, that he was nowhere near the campus on the night of the murder.

Finally, as if the "religious-fanatic theory" of the murder needed additional support, the press duly reported that Mrs. R. M. Russell, wife of the minister who presided at the headmaster's funeral in New Jersey, said that she was inclined to believe that the murder was the work of a maniac, "perhaps a religious maniac." Another representative of organized religion, Reverend W. W. Coe, a retired minister living in East Northfield, visited the headquarters of the investigators and, as the *Times* put it, expounded "at some length" on the reasons he believed that Speer's murderer was a religious fanatic or maniac. Lieutenant Dasey weighed in with his speculation on the same subject: "There may have been other motives," he told the press. "Mr. Speer may have had some enemy about whom we know nothing, but I think, with these people in the village, that religious fanaticism may be behind it."

Big-city reporters, cynical and secular, were no doubt amazed by this school—with its old-fashioned religion and, even after Elliott Speer's modernizing, its restrictive rules. Here was a place that the Roaring Twenties seemed to have missed. Understandably, then, press reports concentrated on the conflict between the "fundamentalists" and the liberalizing Speer.

Lacking physical clues or a suspect, the police, like the reporters, were focused on motives and the possibility that the killer may have been a "maniac" or a "religious fanatic." In an attempt to attach these characteristics to real people connected to the school, particularly students, they approached the school physician, Dr. R. Bretney Miller. On some basis that was not revealed, he delivered the names of five boys who in his opinion had disclosed mental instability. Police were to check where each of the boys was on the night of the murder.

Finally, the police announced that they would begin a search of each home and building on the Mount Hermon campus the following day. If the killer had something hidden in a home on campus, he was thus forewarned and provided an opportunity to hide it elsewhere.

Thursday

～

Classes Begin While the Search Goes On

For the students, 524 of them, classes began. Since the police could no longer use them to help in the search, Lieutenant Dasey arranged to import two hundred boys from the Civilian Conservation Corps (a New Deal program designed to provide work for young men) who had been camped in Erving, Massachusetts, to continue searching the wooded hills on the campus and along the highways leading to the school.

An additional area to be searched was the headmaster's "secret" study over the garage behind Ford Cottage. Police initially felt that the hidden nature of this room showed that Speer feared an attack from his enemies (as they had thought the target pistol in his study inside the residence was evidence of a perceived need for self-defense). Ashtrays and books, however, suggested that the headmaster retreated here to smoke and read in private. He had made it clear when he arrived at Mount Hermon that he did not object to smoking by members of the faculty and administration (who had been forbidden to smoke under the previous headmasters), and even that he did not consider smoking by students (at least seniors) to be a cause for expulsion, so long as it was done discreetly. He was careful, though, to avoid being seen smoking on campus. This garage-study was not only a smoking room, though. It contained files, a couch, a large desk, and well-stocked bookshelves. So there was more to keep the investigators occupied.

The newspapers reported that Dr. Speer, Elliott's father, commented on the theory that his son's killing was the result of changes he had made as headmaster. He strongly expressed his opinion that this was nonsense. "There was no change in the policies of the school when my son became headmaster, as I see it," he said with, perhaps, some exaggeration. "The school's progress has always continued steadily onward."

Friday

∽

No New Clues

The Civilian Conservation Corps boys arrived, complete with their field kitchens and tents. They camped on the edge of the campus and began a foot-by-foot search of the forested campus for the murder weapon.

Lieutenant Dasey spent the day in Brattleboro, Vermont, twenty miles north of the campus. He was there to look into a report that a former resident of that town owed Elliott Speer a large sum of money, which might have provided that person a motive to eliminate him. This lead, like so many others in this case, led nowhere. The debt, it seems, was owed to the Northfield Bank, of which Mr. Speer was a director, not to Speer personally.

The police continued their investigation of boys who had been expelled. This also was destined to come to nothing. One faculty member, echoing the opinion of "Red" Thompson, predicted that this would be the case. "Among the boys who were sent away I do not believe there were any who left with any rancor in their hearts for the headmaster," he said. "Several of them came to me and declared that they had been treated fairly and that Mr. Speer had always been their friend."

The first week of the investigation ended with little progress to show for the efforts of the police: no murder weapon, no eyewitnesses, only speculation as to motive, and no suspect.

The Investigation Continues

The police continued their attempts to solve the crime in the same vein over the following weeks. Various leads were investigated, debunked, and described in the inside pages of the papers, as public attention outside of northern Massachusetts declined or was transferred to other stories, such as that involving Bruno Richard Hauptmann, who had been arrested on September 19 and charged with the kidnapping and murder of the baby son of Charles Lindbergh.

Lieutenant Dasey reported the usual miscellany of tips and rumors to the remaining reporters. A woman said she had seen a young man carrying a shotgun on the Mount Hermon campus on the night of the murder. Another young man, named John Wyatt, told police he had attended Mount Hermon and later worked on a farm in Northfield. He named two local boys he said would know something about the shooting. Bartlett later reported that he had questioned the named boys, but they knew nothing about the shooting. In fact, young Wyatt had never attended Mount Hermon. According to his father, the boy had been suffering from "sleeping sickness" and, said the father, was prone to exaggeration and "romancing."

There was even the inevitable suspicion that the handsome headmaster might have been carrying on an affair with another woman and been killed by a jealous husband. In fact, there was a woman friend who, with her husband, had a summer home in East Northfield. They and the Speers played tennis and bridge together, and she enjoyed riding with Elliott in his convertible with the top down. She was close to him, and even asked his advice on personal matters. But there was no affair, no jealous husband. Her husband said, "Elliott Speer did more for my wife than anyone else could have. It was one of the finest relationships I've ever seen." Police confirmed that the husband had been far away from the campus on the night of the murder, and no one who knew Elliott and Holly Speer ever voiced any suspicion that he would have been unfaithful.

By the end of September, the police said they had interviewed more than 250 people. Dasey made a statement: "We have found it necessary as the result of investigations pursued for the last week to center our present activities close to the Speer household." As we shall see shortly, this statement provided little insight into the actual progress of their work.

5

Dear Elliott and Dear Tom

Dasey's statement implied that the police were back where they had started—not because of the lack of leads, but because all the leads had led into blind alleys. Finally, though, a break had come, from an unexpected source.

At some point during the week of September 24, probably on Thursday the 27th, the district attorney received a call from Wilfred Fry, the president of the schools' board of trustees, asking for a meeting. Fry had, since the Sunday after the shooting, been acting as an amateur detective on the basis of some information he had received that had aroused his suspicions. He had not wanted to share this information with the police until he determined that others knowledgeable about the school's administration supported his suspicions. Finally, he felt he was compelled to turn over this evidence, but he did so reluctantly because the evidence he possessed implicated a trusted member of the Mount Hermon community.

At their meeting, Fry turned over to Bartlett copies of two letters that, he told the district attorney, he had first seen on Sunday morning, September 16. He explained to Bartlett that Dean Elder had showed him the letters immediately before the board of trustees meeting to appoint the committee that would carry on the headmaster's duties following the murder.

Fry described the events that led to his meeting with Elder, from the time he had first learned of Elliott Speer's murder. Dean Elder had called him at about 9:30 on the night of the shooting. Fry had then hurriedly left his summer home in New York and had his chauffeur drive him to East Northfield, arriving at the Northfield Inn about 5:00 Saturday morning. Later, no doubt after offering his condolences to Holly and the Speer family, he went to Holbrook Hall, the administration building on the Mount Hermon campus, and dictated telegrams to the other trustees and then telegrams containing the official death notice to the newspapers. There he was introduced to Bartlett and Lieutenant Dasey. Of course he also wanted to speak with the dean, whose office was in the building. After a few words about the shocking event of the night before, the dean said to Fry, "Now, Wilfred, I suppose the Trustees will want me to carry on just as though Elliott were away for an absence as I always have done. He, as you know, left matters very largely in my hands." The careful Fry did not want to raise any false hopes in Elder's mind, and he responded, "Tom, in the office of dean, yes." Fry also noticed that two of Elder's fingers were bandaged. When he inquired what had happened, Elder dismissed it. "Oh, that is nothing."

Fry was wise not to have implied to the dean that he might be made acting headmaster. The executive committee of the board of trustees, meeting that afternoon, shared his opinion that Elder could not be given that responsibility. Many felt that the dean's health would not permit him to undertake the job. Elder had suffered a serious heart attack a few years earlier and was clearly still not in the best of health. Fry added that "some of us [on the committee] didn't think he was temperamentally or educationally fit for the task." The committee first decided to appoint David Porter, the newly appointed head of the Bible Department, as acting headmaster, but Porter said he would prefer that the job be given to a committee.

Ultimately, on Sunday morning the executive committee decided to create a committee headed by Porter, with Elder and Professor Jackson as the two other members. There was some concern about how to break this to Elder, who many thought would be disappointed. Fry was given the assignment of talking to the dean. So, after the meeting, he telephoned Elder and told him, "Tom, the Executive Committee would like to meet Mr. Porter, yourself and Mr. Jackson in the Board Room [at Holbrook Hall on campus] at quarter to twelve." Elder understood what this meant—he would be part of a committee, not acting headmaster.

"Yes, yes, I'll do that," he answered, "but, Wilfred, I would like to see you for a few minutes before that meeting."

Fry drove over to Holbrook Hall, arriving a little early, and spoke with Elder in his office. He recalled that the dean spoke "rather thickly and haltingly." Obviously in an emotional state, Elder quickly got to the point, "You know, Wilfred, that Elliott always used to leave matters completely in my hands. He used to tell me I could run the school as well as he, or words to that effect."

Nevertheless, Fry broke the news that Elder was dreading: "Tom, the Trustees have decided to appoint a committee." Fry explained that Elder would be a member of the committee, but that Porter would be chairman.

Apparently greatly upset, Elder said, "Well, I would rather resign." Finally, though, after Fry appealed to his loyalty to the school, Elder agreed to serve on the committee "for the present at least." Then, after a pause, he said, "I wonder if I would be breaking Elliott's confidence if I showed you some correspondence that we have had."

Fry sensibly replied, "I do not see how anyone could break Elliott's confidence now."

Elder went on, "You know we used to talk things over very intimately, and back some weeks ago we had a long conference and we agreed to put in writing the results of that conference confirming our impressions each to the other. Here are two letters, my letter to him and his to me." He handed two typewritten letters to Fry, who read them.

THE NORTHFIELD SCHOOLS
MOUNT HERMON SCHOOL   NORTHFIELD SEMINARY
OFFICE OF THE DEAN, MOUNT HERMON SCHOOL
MOUNT HERMON, MASSACHUSETTS

February 18, 1934

Dear Elliott:

At your request I am writing, with reluctance, my understanding of our recent conversation and also reiterating in writing the views which I expressed to you verbally.

First, may I say thank you for the generous statement you made to me relative to increase in salary and certain perquisites to begin next July. You are generous and kind. I am particularly grateful for your gracious offer regarding the pension which you promised in case of a breakdown in my health and for the extension of the pension in part to my wife for her life if I should be taken.

Your earnest request for me to work less is appreciated, but I simply must work. Since I began to work for the schools in the summer of 1900 I have tried to give to the work all that I had. I am glad to believe that I was a help to Dr. Cutler. I am glad that you think I have helped you.

It is hard for me to express my views in writing as I did in our conversation. Somehow it involves sentiment, and while sentiment may clash with logic, it is I think a vital factor in community life and especially in a community so closely interrelated as we are here.

In regard to the Bible courses they bother me. I am, I suppose, what may be called a moderate liberal. There are certain things which the Founder accepted, and which Dr. Cutler said he accepted, that I frankly cannot understand. I am not, however, ready to raise issues of which I am in doubt, nor am I ready to teach youth that the old is not sound. I cannot subscribe to the view that Christ was a good man, as Ghandi [sic] is, and that there is nothing beyond this life. I think it contrary to the very foundation of the principles of the Founder, contrary to the beliefs of your own illustrious father, to the beliefs of John R. Mott, Dr. Grenfell, and to many of the Trustees, particularly to that prince of men, Mr. Bulkley, and others. In my opinion your Bible teachers are wrong in raising doubts in the minds of young boys, those doubts will come all too soon.

I like Les White. Your feeling that he will never be an educator may be true, I cannot say. I do know that his prayer-meetings are good. His Chapel talks, however, I think would be better if he did not cater to the idea that boys should be entertained. I, personally, am not interested in popularity. It is the permanent and not the temporary that interests me most and I firmly believe that boys will later in life appreciate more the teacher, or guide, who works always towards the eternal.

Perhaps it may be well, as you contemplate, to place Mr. Deming in the Cashier's office. He has had no training for that work, but he certainly is not an outstanding teacher. I had hoped he would work into the Study Hall, but he does not seem to understand boys well enough for that. He has a wonderful spirit, however, and his courage under handicaps has been an inspiration to me. I feel badly to have Mr. Koehler go because after all he has done his work well. I do not care to comment on Mr. S. A. You know him. Your idea of keeping him from having much contact with boys and their parents may be wise. I am under the impression, however, that he is not ready for retirement so soon as you hope. I can understand your statements regarding Al. Frankly, I think both you and he are strong personalities that are obliged to clash at times. You think he wants to have too much to say about the affairs of the schools and I am sure he feels the same way regarding you. Perhaps you are both right. It will work out all right in the end. You may recall that I recommended him for the position and I have had no cause to regret it. Of course, the Science Department is weak. It is too bad, for Mr. Barrus is such a good man. We need, however, a forceful, mature, and well-trained man to head that Department. Spurgeon Gage is a wonder, I only wish he had completed his college course.

I think you are making some changes too fast. I personally do not see any improvement in scholarship, even the changes in Crossley have not contributed to higher standards.

Yes, I think you have made mistakes—it was inevitable. I imagine Dr. Cutler made them when he first came. Numerous changes must result in some mistakes and yet it is better to make mistakes than to become stagnant.

I have given you unstinted loyalty, I could do nothing else. I believe in many of the changes you have made, and I further believe that those changes which may not work you will be the first to change them.

It has been a hard year for me. You have, however, been fair and square, it is a joy to work with you. I believe you will go far. You may count on me to the limit of my strength and the utmost of my ability.

Ever yours,

Tom

THE NORTHFIELD SCHOOLS
MOUNT HERMON SCHOOL   NORTHFIELD SEMINARY
OFFICE OF THE HEADMASTER, MOUNT HERMON SCHOOL
MOUNT HERMON, MASSACHUSETTS

February 19, 1934

Dear Tom:

To prevent any misunderstanding and for your own confidential use, I am confirming our recent conversation.

Dr. Cutler once said to me, "I would rather lose any three heads of departments than Tom." After working with you I can make that same statement, not because we agree on all things, but because of your frankness, your loyalty and your executive and administrative ability. You know more about the history, work and need of the school than any man now connected with the work. As I told you, I think you are woefully underpaid and while I cannot begin to offer you what you have been offered by other institutions in the past, I am going to raise your pay beginning next fiscal year as follows:

$4000 per year plus your fuel, electricity and care of your lawn; if at any time you continue to make a fool of yourself by working too hard, as I fear you will, I shall use all my influence with the Trustees to retire you on $3000 per year as long as you live and if you should die before Mrs. Elder, to pay her from the time of your death $1500 a year so long as she lives. I am sure that the Trustees will back me in this when they know how much you have helped both Dr. Cutler and me.

I do not agree with you relative to the Bible Department. In my opinion Les White has a good influence with boys, but he is not and will never be an educator. I think you worry too much about the socialistic tendencies of some of the younger teachers. If they do not believe in immortality, I think they should be honest and teach their convictions. Boys are going to face the question sooner or later—why not now?

I think there has been too much effort to keep the school different from other schools. The Founder and Mr. W. R. are both dead and a new era based on modernistic views is replacing the old. You have been much more liberal than many, but I think you still wish to retain too much of the old. You know perfectly well that that cannot be done.

You may be right in saying I made a mistake in laxity of discipline. I think perhaps you are right—I am drifting somewhat to your point of view, "That proper emphasis on scholarship will take care of most of the discipline of the school."

I think we agree also that the Science Department is in for a shake-up and that I shall have to fire Mr. Barruss.

In the Cashier's office I would like to keep Mr. S. A. from contact with the students as far as possible. Following the plans I talked over with you, I think I shall have to fire Koehler, put Wilson in his place and put Mr. Deming at the desk. Mr. Deming may not be fitted for this position, but you know as well as I that he cannot teach and you think it would be un-christian to throw him out. I expect you, of course, to handle all correspondence with parents and guardians in regard to finance, just as you have been doing this year. I have already told S. A. to turn these matters over to you, which I understand he has done. I shall be glad when S. A. reaches sixty-five, when we shall certainly wish to retire him.

You are all wrong about the tobacco. I think it is all right for the young teachers to smoke. Your idea that they "should not go to classes seeped in tobacco when boys are not permitted to use it" is all bunk!

I hope the advisery [sic] system will work out all right. You will have to father it and we shall have to make changes as the needs arise.

I do not think Al is so valuable as you think. I hired him on your recommendations, but he is too much inclined to think that he runs the school. I want to find a younger man to work into his place and am counting on your help.

We must progress and, frankly, I don't care how soon some of the old teachers get through. They have been helpful, but they are not in line with progressive educational ideas. You are by far the most progressive of them all and I am going to leave more and more of that side of the work to you. I simply must be away from the school more and more as time passes. I have explicit confidence in you personally and in your ability. There is not a single phase of the work that you cannot handle exactly as well as I. We are going to have a good time working out our plans together.

With best wishes,

Not voicing his thoughts after reading the letters, Fry said, "Nevertheless, Tom, we are going to follow out the plan which I have indicated." Then: "May I have these letters? I should like to study over them."

Appearing a little reluctant, Elder said, "Why, yes, if you don't think I am breaking confidence with Elliott."

At the meeting of the executive committee, which took place in Holbrook Hall immediately after Fry and Elder had their talk, Porter, Jackson, and Elder were asked if they were willing to undertake the assignment. All assented, although Elder, very flushed, said, "I have always been carrying the responsibility in the absence of Dr. Cutler and Elliott Speer, but I will accept the task you ask me to do, but I would like to have it understood that my resignation is in your hands and I would like to have it accepted at an early date."

After the meeting, the trustees and the newly appointed committee members proceeded up to Ford Cottage for the memorial service. Now, in addition to the grief he shared with the others who attended that service, Fry was troubled by the letters Elder had given him, and what they might suggest about the murder.

By nature careful and conscientious, Fry wanted to check his first reaction with others before taking the letters to the police. Over the next week, he read parts of the Dear Tom letter to others who had been close to Elliott Speer. He was particularly troubled by the last paragraph, which contained the sentence "There is not a single phase of the work that you cannot handle exactly as well as I." He doubted that Speer would have written that. The first time he read that sentence, in Dean Elder's office, he had thought, "If Elliott wrote this letter to Elder he didn't play square with me." He read the same paragraph to Fred Newton, who was the president of the Alumni Association and chairman of the executive committee of the board of trustees. Newton, who knew Elliott Speer well, said the paragraph was "strange." Fry later said that it was at this point that he had a "jolt." He said aloud, "Great Scott! The thing isn't signed!" Then he remembered that Elder might have mentioned something about the letters being copies.

Later that week, having made his own copies of the letters (by a stenographer—this was long before photocopying), he mailed them back to Elder. Fry wondered whether the increase of Elder's salary to $4,000 a year promised in the third paragraph of the Dear Tom letter had really been put in place. So, in the cover letter returning the letters to Elder he asked, "Am I right in assuming that the arrangements made for an increase in compensation were carried into effect last July?" Responding in a letter dated September 20, Elder wrote him, "You were not right in assuming that arrangements regarding compensation were carried into effect last July. It slipped Elliott's attention and he talked with me afterwards."

Fry was coming to doubt the genuineness of the Dear Tom letter. He recognized that if the letter were not genuine it would have had no value to Dean Elder while Elliott Speer was alive. Increasingly troubled, Fry called an old acquaintance, a detective named William Houghton, and asked to meet with him. Houghton was an agent for the United States Secret Service and had been involved in a number of important investigations, including the Teapot Dome scandal, and had done some spectacular work against German spies in World War I. The records do not reveal how Fry came to be acquainted with him.

Houghton came to Fry's office in Philadelphia early on Monday, September 24. Fry had Houghton read the letters, after giving him the necessary background information. He explained why he had been reluctant to show the letters to the police. "Please recognize the very embarrassing position in which I may be placed and the schools may be placed," he said to Houghton, "if I reveal these letters to anyone—this possibly reflecting upon a member of the faculty and quite likely upon an innocent man." Houghton and Fry did not decide at this meeting what to do about the letters.

While he was thinking about Elder, Fry recalled hearing that Elder had been the first person to telephone Ford Cottage after the shooting. His curiosity on this point may have been triggered by an article in the September 18 issue of the *Greenfield (Massachusetts) Recorder Gazette*. The article, riddled with errors, was headlined "Phone Call Killer Clew." Subheads reported that "Excited Voice Asked for Speer after Murder" and announced a "Theory Telephone Was Used by Slayer Who Wondered Whether Aim Was Fatal."

To confirm that Elder had indeed called Ford Cottage shortly after the shooting, Fry asked Mira Wilson, the principal of the Northfield Seminary and a close friend of Speer, to find out about the incident. Of course, he did not tell her why he was interested. She reported back to Fry that Dean Elder had indeed called Ford Cottage shortly after the shooting and had insisted on speaking to "Elliott" until he was told that Speer had been shot and was dead.

This prompted Fry to ask Houghton to meet with him again. At that meeting, Houghton told him that the only course for him to pursue was to turn over the letters to the district attorney.

Fry remained very reluctant to do this, out of concern for the reputation of Elder as well as that of the school. So he traveled to Boston to discuss again his suspicions and the letters with Fred Newton, the chairman of the executive committee, who told Fry he hoped he could delay turning over the letters. Next, Fry met with John Grandin, another member of the executive committee. Grandin was a hard-headed businessman who now lived in Boston, but he had made his money in lumbering in the South and Northwest, in oil production in Louisiana and Pennsylvania, and in wheat farming in the Red River Valley of North Dakota.

At this meeting, at the Ritz Hotel in Boston on Wednesday, September 26, Fry showed Grandin the letters for the first time. Grandin told Fry that he had discussed Dean Elder with Elliott Speer several times. Speer had told him that he would like to have

Elder retire. Grandin told Fry that Speer had said he believed Elder's heart condition resulted in a nervous temperament and that Elder "was a problem and he should be eliminated from the work." Grandin read the Dear Tom letter, and he later testified as follows: "I was shocked. I was more than surprised. The first impression that came to me was that Elliott Speer could not have written that letter." Particularly troublesome to Grandin was the sentence in the letter in which the letter's author, purportedly Speer, wrote, "I simply must be away from the school more and more as time passes." This did not correspond with Grandin's recollection. "One point the trustees had talked with Elliott Speer about, and one thing he craved, was to be more on the job. We didn't want him running around raising money. He wanted to be in close contact with the boys."

Grandin decided to go with Fry to Northfield the next day to meet with District Attorney Bartlett. Fry also called Houghton and asked him to come up to Northfield and join them. (Fry had told Bartlett that the trustees would not interfere with his investigation, so he wanted to introduce Houghton to Bartlett and get Bartlett's permission for him to be involved.)

So, on September 27, Fry and Grandin (and, apparently, Houghton) met with Bartlett and turned the copies of the letters over to him. Later, Fry met with Elliott's parents and Holly. He did not, however, disclose the existence of the letters to them. When he asked Holly about her husband's relationship with the dean, she told him that "Elliott had found Elder difficult." Fry asked Dr. Speer, who had been reading his son's diary, what Elliott had been doing around the middle of February—the Dear Tom letter was dated February 19. According to Dr. Speer, Elliott had been in Philadelphia on Saturday, the 17th, arrived home on the night of the 18th (the date of the Dear Elliott letter from Elder) and, according to the diary, had a busy day on the 19th. Fry wondered how he could have found time to write a long letter during that period.

The next day, September 28, Fry and Grandin had a busy day assisting the investigators. They met again with Bartlett in Greenfield and then met with Gordon McEwan, Mount Hermon's assistant treasurer. McEwan confirmed what Fry had learned from

Elder, that the dean's salary had not been raised in the amount purportedly agreed upon in the Dear Tom letter. Later, Fry met with Mira Wilson, the Northfield Seminary principal, and read the Dear Tom letter to her. She told him, emphatically, that her friend Elliott Speer could not have written it.

Fry was ill and must have been exhausted, though he might not have been aware that he was suffering from cancer. As he was about to head for the train station to go back to Philadelphia, he received a call from Elder, who wanted to meet with him. Fry invited the dean to come to the Northfield Inn to meet with him and Grandin. There, Elder told the two trustees that he had been talking with Bartlett and had turned the letters over to him. He asked Fry, once again, if he felt that he had broken a confidence with Speer. Fry then advised Elder that he had already told Bartlett about the letters and that he was glad that Elder had turned them over. Grandin asked Elder if the letters were originals. The dean said, "No. The originals were in ink, and I destroyed Elliott's because of its very confidential nature, and I do not know where mine is, possibly in Elliott's files." Elder said he had made pencil copies and had dictated from those to a stenographer, but he could not remember where. He had not dictated them to his own secretary because, he said, he had felt the letters were too confidential. Grandin then asked "how he came to have [the Dear Tom letter] copied on the Headmaster's paper." Elder told them that he "used the Headmaster's paper at times." The meeting ended with both Grandin and Fry unsatisfied—in fact, more suspicious than before.

Elder, of course, had not been aware when he met with Bartlett that afternoon that the district attorney had already seen the letters. Bartlett had wanted to see if Elder would give him these letters voluntarily. Accordingly, he had asked Elder if there was any correspondence at the schools that might shed some light on plans to dismiss people, or the like. The dean told him that he had already made all correspondence available to the investigators. Bartlett had to push a little harder. "I have heard somewhere, or I have the impression somehow that you and Elliott had some correspondence back some months ago which related to people and the

THIS BOOK BELONGS TO THE
VAN BUREN PUBLIC LIBRARY

policy in the schools. I may be wrong about that, but I have that impression."

The dean, perhaps suspicious that Bartlett knew more than he was saying, reluctantly admitted, "Well, there was some correspondence, but it was of a very confidential nature and it would be of no help to you."

Bartlett asked where that correspondence was.

"At my home," said Elder.

Bartlett asked the dean to get the letters, and they drove together over to Elder's house on the lower level of the campus, near the farm. Elder retrieved them and gave them to the district attorney, but grudgingly. "I hate to give these to you as they are very confidential."

Bartlett read the letters (again—he had already read the copies Fry and Grandin had turned over to him) and said, "Why, Tom, the letter from Elliott to you isn't signed."

Elder told him, "No, Joe. That's a copy, that's a copy. Elliott asked me to destroy the original."

Bartlett asked the obvious question, "But the letter from you to Elliott is the original, is it?"

"Yes."

"That came from Elliott's files?"

"Yes, that came from Elliott's files." But the dean quickly amended that answer. "This letter of mine to Elliott, Elliott handed back to me after he read it." Later that night, Elder called Bartlett at his home, to again change his version. He said both the letters were copies, each having been originally written in longhand. He went on: "Something you didn't understand or that I didn't tell you was that the reason I had that copy of Elliott Speer's letter to me made was because there was a paragraph in there about Dr. Cutler which Elliott didn't want preserved, either in the original or the copies." Bartlett asked where he had had the copies made, but Elder said he could not remember.

By this point, Dean Elder had given several versions of the history of the letters. When he first showed them to Fry, just before the trustees met to decide who should run the school, he may have said they were copies. Later, he told Bartlett that only the

Dear Tom letter was a copy, and that the Dear Elliott letter had been returned to him by Speer and was the original, then that both were copies. Still later, he told Bartlett that Speer had told him to destroy the original of the Dear Tom letter because it contained uncomplimentary references to Dr. Cutler, Speer's predecessor. In addition, Bartlett knew by this time that the salary increase promised in the Dear Tom letter had not been given to Elder. No doubt he also was aware of other reasons to doubt the genuineness of that letter: that Elliott Speer's diary did not mention any such discussion or letter; that, on the contrary, the schedule revealed in the diary suggested that he did not have time on February 19, the date of the purported letter, to write it; and that close associates of the headmaster, including Fry and Grandin, felt, from its contents, that Elliott Speer could not have written it.

Still other questions could be raised: Why did Dean Elder copy the Dear Tom letter on the headmaster's stationery? Was it likely he would destroy the signed original of a letter promising him a substantial salary increase and a pension? Why was neither copy so labeled? Why was no omission indicated to show the deletion of the unfavorable material about Dr. Cutler in the Dear Tom copy? And most important, though unprovable perhaps, did the Dear Tom letter display Speer's style, and would Speer have been likely to have written such a frank letter to Elder? If Elder had fabricated the Dear Tom letter, as Bartlett surely believed, how could the district attorney prove that beyond a reasonable doubt? On the other hand, if it could be proved that Elder had forged the letter, he was likely Speer's killer—the letter would be useless to him while Speer was alive.

At last, a real suspect had emerged.

6

Pressuring the Suspect

Houghton, the Secret Service agent who had been asked by Fry to assist the Massachusetts authorities, was still in town, and Bartlett brought him along the next day to help in questioning Elder. Bartlett introduced him to Elder, for some reason, as "Mr. Jones, a friend of mine." Elder was not fooled, and he immediately took a strong dislike to the aggressive detective as it became apparent to him, probably for the first time, that he was the prime suspect in the murder of Elliott Speer.

The questioning, primarily by Houghton, was decidedly unfriendly. He asked the obvious questions about the Dear Tom letter: Where were the copies made? Elder could not remember. Were the two letters copied by different stenographers? Yes. How did it happen that the Dear Tom letter was copied on the headmaster's stationery? Elder said he always carried that stationery with him. Houghton obviously did not believe Elder's story, saying at one point, "No twelve men would ever believe that story. You are talking yourself right into jail."

The questioning by Bartlett and Houghton was not limited to the letters. They even suggested that the old dean's relationship with his secretary, the young and trim Evelyn Dill, was improper.

Houghton asked Elder directly if he was "familiar" with his secretary, and whether Speer had ever spoken to him about it. Of his relationship with Miss Dill, Elder admitted only that he took her for rides in his car, and he told Houghton that Speer had never criticized him about it.

Unable to get Elder to change his story, the district attorney and Houghton returned to the Bernardston Inn, a few miles down the road from the campus, where the investigators had set up their headquarters, and briefed the other detectives for the first time about the letters. One of them, excited to finally have a suspect, said of Elder, "Let's go lock him up."

Bartlett resisted that advice, and it wasn't until the night of October 5, almost a week later, that a real attempt was made to break Elder. In the interim, Bartlett and the detectives reviewed all the evidence, including the witness interviews that had been gathered so far, with an eye to how they reflected on the dean. Where was he at the time of the killing? What would his motive have been for killing Speer? Did he ever own a 12-gauge shotgun and know how to use it?

October 5, 1934

On October 5, Elder was attending an evening meeting at Holbrook Hall when he received a call from Bartlett, who asked if he could come and talk with him. The dean said he was quite tired, but he ultimately agreed. He was surprised when six detectives showed up, with a stenographer, but without Bartlett. Elder protested again that he was tired and would prefer not to be questioned, but the detectives, led by John Stokes, were insistent. Questioning began about 10:00 P.M. in the headmaster's office.

The first question was whether Elder had retained an attorney. Elder said that he had not, but that he had spoken with attorney Charles Fairhurst of Greenfield after he had been questioned by Bartlett and "Mr. Jones."

Then the questioning focused on the Dear Tom letter. Elder told the detectives that in February or March he and the headmaster had been discussing the faculty, and Speer had said he felt some of the teachers should not be retained. Elder said Speer had asked him to put his thoughts on the matter in writing. Both he and Speer wrote their letters in longhand, he said. He could not remember where he had the copies made—he had dictated them to a stenographer—or whether he had both copies made at the same time. He said he remembered, though, that he had left out a portion of Speer's Dear Tom letter that referred to Dr. Cutler.

Questioned about his actions on the night of the shooting, Elder said he had had supper with his wife at his home. Afterward, his wife was folding some campaign letters on the dining room table—Elder was running for local office. He told the detectives that he had then driven his car to Northfield to have a headlight replaced at Morgan's Garage, then had returned to the campus. He said he had parked near Holbrook Hall at about 7:40. The detectives wanted to know whether anyone had seen him when he arrived at Holbrook Hall. Elder said he had noticed a couple of boys working there when he entered, but did not know whether they had seen him. Then, he said, he had gone to his office, where he remained until almost 9:00. Since the shooting took place at about 8:20 that evening, this version, if corroborated, would clear the dean.

Throughout this long interrogation, which lasted into early morning, there were breaks in the questioning during which the detectives called in others who might be able to contradict or corroborate Elder's story—apparently without regard to the lateness of the hour. For example, they called in Miss Lovell, Elliott Speer's secretary, to ask whether he had been in the habit of writing letters in longhand. She said that he never did in the office, to her knowledge, only occasionally writing personal letters to his family in longhand. She also said she had never seen any letter written in longhand by Speer to Elder.

The same technique was employed by the detectives when Elder was questioned about his ownership of a 12-gauge shotgun. He told them that he had owned such a gun many years ago in Virginia but that it had been destroyed in a fire. He admitted owning the 20-gauge gun he had previously turned over to the police,

Holbrook Hall, where Speer, Elder, and Norton had their offices.
Author's photo.

but he denied ever having a 12-gauge gun at Mount Hermon since he came to work there in 1900. The detectives then brought in Daniel Van Valkenburgh, the school's blacksmith, to repeat a story he had previously told them: that he had been hunting with Elder at Mount Hermon and that Elder had used what Van Valkenburgh recalled was a 12-gauge shotgun.

Elder remained unflustered. He calmly told the detectives, "I haven't the remotest recollection of what he is talking about at all. I don't remember hunting with him, but if he says so, it must be true."

The questioners returned again and again to the Dear Tom letter. Had the dean been in the habit of carrying the headmaster's stationery with him when he traveled? Yes, "his and mine." Suspecting that Elder might have typed the Dear Tom letter himself after the shooting, the detectives asked him if he, or anyone in his family, knew how to type. No, answered the dean, and he did not have a typewriter at home, his wife did not type, and his son, who was at college, "types abominably." Elder told the detectives that he had destroyed the original of the Dear Tom letter, as he had consistently maintained, and added that he had also destroyed other personal letters from Speer after the shooting.

Elder seems to have remained calm and alert throughout the many hours of this interrogation. He refused to answer only one question. He was asked, "Was it ever called to your attention at any time during your existence here about a peek hole?" He said, "I prefer not to discuss that without counsel." (This "peek hole" became important in a later proceeding. See Chapter 10.) The questioning finally ended at 4:15 in the morning of October 6.

In the small community of Mount Hermon it was soon common knowledge that Dean Elder had been questioned in Holbrook Hall by a team of detectives through the night. A rumor swept the school that he had been arrested. Several people called his house on the morning of October 6 to learn if that was true.

The dean wrote to Wilfred Fry complaining that the letters he had showed to Fry had resulted in his interrogation.

> I feel very keenly, and it grieves me deeply, to know that it was felt necessary to send private detectives to Mount Hermon to investigate [the letters]. These letters I later turned over to the District Attorney without any compulsion. The methods used by these detectives were, I think, wholly unfair and unjust. I was thoroughly exhausted by the tragedy which affected me deeply and then to be questioned from between nine and ten o'clock in the evening of one day until 4:30 in the morning of the next day by seven men was, I feel, very unjust. I have nothing to conceal, but I do resent the unfair methods used.

Mrs. Speer, shortly after the night of questioning, also heard the rumor that the dean was a suspect. She had not been briefed about the status of the investigation, nor had she yet seen the Dear Tom letter. Feeling that the dean could not have been guilty of murdering her husband, she went down to the Elders' house to visit him. She later said, "I felt I could at least do that much for him in the eyes of the campus." She recalled that Elder was "nervous and blustery" and "very much excited." He asked her, characteristically, whether she didn't think he had a good alibi, having been in Holbrook Hall at the time of the shooting. In fact Elder, throughout the period after the killing, appeared to be concerned exclusively with his own problems, oblivious even to the grief of Holly Speer. He had asked her, shortly after she had returned to campus following her husband's funeral, whether Elliott had ever said anything against him. On the same occasion, Elder told the recently widowed young woman, "I am going through such a terrible thing." At the inquest in December, Mrs. Speer testified that this comment left her "a little bit surprised, because I had been trying not to think of myself in this thing, but I felt I had been going through a good deal, too." She had said to Elder, "I have been going through some things myself." She remembered "quite a look of surprise on his face."

By this time, when the police had decided that Elder was the killer, or at least was involved in the killing, the case had virtually disappeared from the newspapers. So, while the rest of the world was forgetting about the crime, the police and the members of the Mount Hermon community knew that a breakthrough had occurred. All eyes at the school were on the dean.

After his questioning by the detectives, it was evident that the dean could no longer function effectively on campus, and, at the request of the trustees, Elder took a leave of absence. His poor health was the reason given publicly.

Others, however, unaware of the breakthrough in the case, continued to provide "tips" to the investigators. In a letter sent to the Northfield Schools (and duly forwarded to the police) in November, a Mr. Wilson advised:

> I am convinced, and felt this way from the first, that he was killed by outsiders who came there for the purpose, and as a result of Dr. Elliott [sic] having dismissed some student. One paper stated the student at the time he was expelled had threatened to GET EVEN. This student was probably planted in that school on purpose to make trouble or spread communism and rebellion among the other students. . . . Communists have planted such so-called students in all institutions over the country.

7

The Inquest

❧

December 3, 1934

◦◦

Dr. Speer and Holly Speer

District Attorney Bartlett decided to ask for an inquest—a judicial examination of the evidence to decide whether Elliott Speer had been murdered (a foregone conclusion) and whether there was sufficient evidence of the identity of the killer or killers to send the case to a grand jury. Judge Timothy Hayes of Greenfield presided when the proceeding began on December 3, 1934, in the new Franklin County courthouse in Greenfield, ten miles south of the campus.

The first question to be decided was whether the inquest should be open to the public or secret. Bartlett argued that it should be secret and that each witness should testify out of the presence of the others. (This is the typical procedure followed in grand jury investigations to this day.) He told Judge Hayes that secrecy would allow each witness to speak freely and would also reduce the chances of "temptation on the part of any party who might be involved criminally to leave the jurisdiction." Hayes granted the district attorney's request.

There is a hint in the transcript that this had been agreed upon beforehand. At one point, when a witness referred to the headmaster's office in Holbrook Hall, the judge asked Bartlett, "Where you and I met Mr. Porter?" It is likely that the school would have preferred that the inquest be held in secret to avoid further publicity and to protect the dean in case the court's decision was not to charge him. Bartlett and Judge Hayes probably met with Porter, the acting headmaster, as a matter of courtesy to discuss the procedure to be followed and to indicate to Porter what witnesses might be called from the school.

With the announcement of the inquest, the case again attracted newspaper coverage. The reporters quickly learned the identity of the chief suspect, but they were unable to name him in print for fear of libel suits. Thus the dean was not identified publicly as a suspect, although his status was common knowledge in the area. The *New York Times*, for example, reported that the chief suspect—unnamed—"had a long conference with his attorney today [December 2] after returning to Northfield to end a month's absence."

The first witnesses called by Bartlett set the scene. A civil engineer presented a map of the Mount Hermon campus, and a photographer described his photographs of the crime scene, which were marked as exhibits. Several faculty witnesses were then called to testify that they had seen the headmaster alive on the afternoon of September 14 in a meeting of the French Department at Holbrook Hall.

Dean Elder testified briefly at this point, primarily to locate his home on the map of the campus.

He was followed on the stand by Elliott Speer's father, Dr. Robert E. Speer. The intense, handsome, gray-haired witness testified persuasively about the reasons he felt that the Dear Tom letter had been forged. He told the judge that, after having examined the letter, he had written to Wilfred Fry, the president of the board of trustees, detailing the reasons he had reached that conclusion. Bartlett established Dr. Speer's qualifications for making that judgment by having him detail the correspondence he had received from his son over the years. Dr. Speer testified that his son had written to his parents almost weekly during his studies at Phillips Andover preparatory school, during his years at Princeton, and when Elliott had been overseas, either studying in Edinburgh or serving with the YMCA. In addition, Dr. Speer had undertaken his own investigation. He said that he had reviewed all of his son's correspondence files, except the official school files, and had found no handwritten letter dated February 18, 1934, from Elder. On the genuineness of the Dear Tom letter, Dr. Speer's opinions were clear, and he stated them emphatically. First, he said that from a purely practical standpoint it was "inconceivable to me that the original letter could have been destroyed with the assurances that it contained, and that the receiver of it [Elder] could have been satisfied by substituting for it a typewritten copy of only a portion of it without any signature attached." In other words, if your boss promised you a large raise and a generous pension in writing, would you destroy the written promise with your boss's signature, and make only a partial, unsigned copy of the letter?

In addition, Dr. Speer testified that he had carefully examined his son's diaries or journals for the period surrounding the time of the supposed conversation with Elder and the writing of the letter, and, he told the district attorney and the judge, "I can't see where there was time for him to have written as long a document as that by his own hand." Moreover, the journals, he said, showed that Elliott Speer was away from campus for three days before the dates of the letters, and the journals appeared to refer to all significant conversations during that period. There was no record in the diaries of any conversation of the type reflected in the letter with Dean Elder. Dr. Speer continued that the Dear Tom letter "contains opinions which we know [Elliott] did not hold." In particular, Dr. Speer testified that his son had not been indifferent "as to whether the teachers taught immortality or not." Finally, with respect to the relationship between his son and the dean, "Elliott was doing his very best for and with Mr. Elder. I think he regarded him as a liability which he had inherited from Dr. Cutler's administration."

S. Allen Norton, the treasurer of the school, and the "S. A." referred to in the Dear Tom letter, testified next. Years later Norton was to become an important figure in the case, but at the inquest his evidence was limited to the question of whether Dean Elder ever received the salary increase promised in the letter. Norton testified that the records showed that Elder received an increase of $120 per month in July of 1934, making his total salary $3,600 annually (not the $4,000 promised in the Dear Tom letter). Norton also testified that only the headmaster received free fuel, electricity, and care of his lawn—again, contrary to the ostensible promise in the Dear Tom letter that the dean would enjoy these benefits.

Next came the very compelling testimony of Holly Speer, Elliott's widow. She, unlike her father-in-law, Dr. Speer, had not yet seen the Dear Tom letter. Her testimony shows vividly how her reading of that letter for the first time on the witness stand upset her and changed her opinion of Dean Elder.

Under the respectful questioning of Bartlett, she first described moving to Northfield when Elliott became president of the schools in 1926; the year in Scotland from September 1931 to July 1932, when Elliott returned with her and the children to become headmaster of Mount Hermon; then the summer vacation of the family on Lake Timagami in Canada. She said the family returned to campus late Sunday night, September 9.

She then described the day of September 14. She had, she said, spent much of the day making visits in East Northfield to take flowers to people who were ill, and she had not returned to Ford Cottage until about 5:30. Elliott had not yet arrived home. As she was finishing dressing for dinner, he came in, took a bath, and got dressed. Meanwhile, Holly went upstairs to spend some time with the children, settled the youngest, and then went down for dinner at 7:00, the usual time the Speers dined.

Immediately after dinner, the Speers and Mr. Welles (Holly's father) discussed playing bridge. Mrs. Welles, being in somewhat poor health, was in the second-floor bedroom (directly over the headmaster's study), and Holly went up to ask if she wanted to play. She did not feel up to it, so Holly began getting her ready for the night. Elliott had gone into his study, while Mr. Welles was reading in the drawing room across the hall.

Holly testified that she heard an "explosion" and Elliott crying out—"a distressed cry . . . more shock than pain." She ran down the stairs saying, "What is it, Elliott?" He said, "I don't know" as he staggered out of the study into the hall, at the bottom of the stairs, with blood dripping from his sleeve. Mr. Welles had also run into the hall. When Holly and her father reached Elliott, she testified, he collapsed into their arms. They laid him on the floor in the hall. Elliott said, "Put a tourniquet on my arm." Holly had been calling for Mrs. George, the maid, to help. Elliott said to send for a doctor. They sent for Dr. McCastline, who lived nearby, and then Holly asked her father to call their friend David Birdsall. Elliott Speer never spoke again.

Holly's testimony continued. While they were still working over the dying headmaster, David Birdsall arrived and quickly decided to call the police. Holly recalled that she had not until then realized "that it was a case for the police. Such a thing never entered my mind until we got Mr. Speer's clothing loosened. Then I realized it was, but even then I couldn't seem to get it through my head that we should get the police. I thought we must do everything for him because I thought perhaps our efforts would save his life, what we could do until the doctor came."

Bartlett asked her whether it had been Elliott's habit to go into the study after dinner. She told him, "Almost as regularly as clockwork, as soon as we had supper, as we had finished, he always went into the study. Often it was his only chance to sit down with the paper. And then he did a little work, and if he could, he tried to play a little bridge with the family before they went upstairs, and they always went to bed earlier than he. He worked very late."

"Where would he sit?"

"Well, if he had work to do, if he was going to work, he would sit at his desk, facing out [the window facing north], and all the books he would be using would be exactly behind him—he was very methodical—his new books and the books he was using, so he wouldn't need to get up to reach them."

Then Bartlett asked Mrs. Speer about her husband's reading habits: "What was his recreational reading?"

"Detective stories, when he was tired."

Bartlett asked when Elliott had purchased the detective novel, *The Public School Murder*. She thought it was about a year before. "I remember Mr. Speer recommending it to me. 'If you want a good story, that's a good story.'"

Did Speer lend his books?

Yes, very freely, "so freely that I began to keep a little list of the books that went out, a little note book, with the exception of some of the detective stories, which I didn't value very much." She said that Elliott often would drop off three or four books if someone was not feeling well.

"To whom on the campus did he lend them?"

"To Mr. Elder because he was ill so much." She recalled, "Mr. Speer would say, 'Tom isn't feeling well. He has gone home, and I will drop him a few detective stories. He is having some sort of heart attack.' He had a bad heart, and so Mr. Speer loaned more books to Mr. Elder of this type." But there was no reference in her "little book" to lending *The Public School Murder* to anyone, including the dean.

She had reviewed her husband's diary for the date of February 19, 1934, the date of the Dear Tom letter. It showed that he had been in the office from 10:00 to 11:00, in committee meetings from 11:00 to 1:00, in Greenfield from 2:00 to 3:00, then in the office again until supper. There was no reference to writing such a letter, which Holly had still not seen.

Then Bartlett asked her to read the two letters. He and Judge Hayes waited silently while she intently read the Dear Tom and Dear Elliott letters.

Her first reaction to the Dear Tom letter was that the phraseology "is not Mr. Speer's." "A good deal of the vocabulary," she said, "is not his, and it's very unusual for Mr. Speer to begin a paragraph with 'I'."

Continuing through the Dear Tom letter, she was adamant that it was not her husband's view, as expressed in the letter, that he would "be away from the school more and more as time passes."

One of the main reasons he wanted to take the headmaster's job and resign the presidency of the schools, she said, was that he could spend more time at home with his family.

Of the statement in the letter "There is not a single phase of the work that you cannot handle exactly as well as I," she recalled:

> A year ago this October Mr. Speer and I had a rare thing, a holiday together one day, walking on the Green Mountain Trail. He was very preoccupied that day, and suddenly he turned to me—a thing he doesn't often do because he has kept all the unpleasant things from me that he could—he said to me, "What am I to do about Tom?" I said, "What do you mean?" And he said, "I don't know how I can go on as things are." And I said, "Why Elliott?" He said, "Well, I think it's illness, but he makes it very difficult for me." I said, "Elliott, I don't think, with all you carry, you should have as dean anyone who in any way makes things difficult. That isn't co-operation." He said, "Well, he has given very faithful service and he is sick, but I don't know what's the right thing to do."

She also recalled that Wilfred Fry, the president of the board of trustees, had said to Elliott, "We know Mr. Elder is difficult. We ask you to play along with him for a while."

As to the sentence in the letter "We are going to have a good time working out our plans together," she testified that it was inconsistent with what Elliott felt: "Because I don't think anyone could have had a good time working with Mr. Elder in his state of health. He was so jumpy and nervous. The phraseology and words aren't my husband's, that's all." She continued, summarizing her feelings having just read the Dear Tom letter for the first time, "I must say I haven't seen this letter [before] and it's upset me a little because it's so absolutely foreign to him."

Bartlett then told Mrs. Speer that Elder claimed that he had left out of the copy of the letter disparaging remarks that Speer had written about Dr. Cutler. "That would be quite impossible," she told him, "because my husband didn't make disparaging remarks about people. . . . I have never heard a criticism of Dr. Cutler [from Elliott]." Moreover, she went on, "Dean Elder would be the last person, if there was any criticism, that my husband would take it to."

The judge asked her to identify "S. A.," referred to in the letter. Mrs. Speer said it referred to S. A. Norton, the school's cashier. Then he asked her if she felt her husband would have written the sentence "I shall be glad when S. A. reaches sixty-five, when we shall certainly wish to retire him." She was very clear he would not have written it. "I am quite sure," she said, "not to Mr. Elder, because there was no feeling of friendliness between those two men, and Mr. Elder would be the last person he would say that to." She said Elliott thought that "Norton was a good routine man but no help in relation to the boys, just a routine man."

She then described the contacts she had had with Elder after the shooting, including the time when she had visited him at his house after hearing the rumor that he was a suspect. "I felt I must if possible give him some support because I felt he was being very unjustly accused. I couldn't dream of such a possibility [that he had murdered her husband], and I have been thinking along those lines, you see, until I saw those letters. I hadn't seen these letters."

At this point, Judge Hayes adjourned the hearing, asking Mrs. Speer to continue her testimony the next day.

December 4, 1934

◁⟫

Wilfred Fry

In the morning, Mrs. Speer returned to the stand, where Bartlett's questions again concerned the Dear Tom letter. He asked her to comment on the sentences in the letter "You may be right in saying I made a mistake in laxity of discipline. I think perhaps you are right—I am drifting somewhat to your point of view." She was emphatic: "My husband didn't drift. That word he would never have used. He did a thing or thought a thing, or he did not think it or did not do it."

Her final comment on the letter dealt with words that were considered slang—and inappropriate to use in writing—at the time: "fire" (instead of "dismiss") and "bunk." "I have never heard my husband use such phrases, and certainly, in writing I know that he just wouldn't have expressed himself in that way."

Although the order of the witnesses after the first day is not clear (the numbered volumes of the transcript, for some reason, are not in chronological order), it appears that the next witness was Wilfred W. Fry, the president of the school's board of trustees. The successful businessman, president of a large advertising firm, was square-jawed and handsome.

Under Bartlett's questioning, Fry recounted the events of the weekend following September 14. He had arrived early on Saturday morning (the 15th) at the Northfield Inn. After breakfast he had his driver take him to the campus, where he met Dean Elder in the dean's office in Holbrook Hall. He still recalled "vividly" the dean's opening comment, "Now, Wilfred, I suppose the Trustees will want me to carry on just as though Elliott were away for an absence as I always have done. He, as you know, left matters very largely in my hands." Looking back, Fry recognized that this was when his suspicions about the dean began.

The Dear Tom letter, which Elder showed him the next day, certainly increased Fry's unease about the dean, but the thought that Elder could have been involved in murdering Elliott Speer was simply too incredible for Fry to entertain at that point.

Over the next week, Fry testified, he selectively disclosed portions of the Dear Tom letter to others. First, after the memorial service at Ford Cottage on Sunday, he read the last paragraph of the letter to Fred Newton, the chairman of the Alumni Association and of the board's executive committee. That paragraph includes the crucial sentences: "I simply must be away from the school more and more as time passes. I have explicit confidence in you personally and in your ability. There is not a single phase of the work that you cannot handle exactly as well as I." Newton commented to Fry that he thought it was a "strange paragraph." Fry then wondered aloud whether Elliott Speer had ever written that. Newton replied, "If he did, he didn't convey the same idea that he did to me in his conversation regarding his problems at Mount Hermon." Newton told Fry that Speer had told him that "Elder was a problem."

Continuing his private investigation, Fry testified, he had read both letters to Edwin Bulkley, another member of the board. Fry chose him because "I felt no man outside of Elliott Speer's family was closer to him than Mr. Bulkley." Bulkley echoed Newton's opinion, after hearing the Dear Tom letter, that parts of it were "strange," particularly the portion in which Speer purportedly wrote that teachers should feel free to teach their convictions if they did not believe in immortality.

Next, Fry testified that he had returned the letters (after having had copies made) to Elder. In the cover letter to the dean he asked whether he had received the salary increase promised in the Dear Tom letter. Elder had replied that he had not received the raise. "It had slipped Elliott's attention," he had written Fry.

In the week following the killing, Fry told Bartlett and Judge Hayes, "the genuineness of [the letter] grew, as I pondered it, increasingly improbable in my mind." Fry recognized at this point, though he might not have been able to say it, that if the dean had forged that letter, he was the obvious suspect in the killing. So he had called Mira Wilson, the headmistress, or principal, of the Northfield Seminary. Without revealing his suspicion, he asked her to find out the "story of the telephoning that was done from the Headmaster's house that night [September 14], how the police were summoned, etc." He was trying to find out where Elder had been when Elliott Speer had been shot, and whether it was true that the dean had been the first person to call Ford Cottage after the shooting. Since Elder had called him from Ford Cottage only an hour after the murder, Fry wondered when the dean had arrived at the headmaster's residence and how he had learned of the crime. Miss Wilson looked into the matter, in a discreet way no doubt, and told Fry (he testified): "As near as I can tell you the story is as follows: . . . that after the murder had occurred, Dean Elder telephoned the house and stated that he would like to speak with Elliott. Mr. Welles answered the telephone and told him that Mr. Speer could not come to the telephone just then. Mr. Elder was very insistent. . . . Mr. Elder insisted that he must speak to him and must speak to him at once." Finally, Miss Wilson told Fry, Welles had informed Elder that Speer had been shot and was dead.

Fry's own suspicions had now been reinforced by Mira Wilson's report and the agreement of two of his colleagues that the Dear Tom letter was at least "strange." He recognized that he could not hold the letters in confidence any longer. He became, he testified, "increasingly uncomfortable and perplexed because it looked to me as though something had been going on which was not straight." So, he arranged to meet at his office with the investigator William Houghton (the Secret Service agent), to satisfy himself that his suspicions were not unreasonable. After hearing Fry's story and reviewing the letters, Houghton told him that he must turn the letters over to the district attorney.

Even after he had delivered the letters to Bartlett, Fry testified, he had continued his personal investigation. He and fellow board member John Grandin met with Gordon McEwan in the Mount Hermon treasurer's office. McEwan told them what the increase in Dean Elder's salary had been—it was not in the amount promised in the Dear Tom letter.

Later, Fry continued, he had read the Dear Tom letter to Mira Wilson at Northfield. She had been hired by Elliott Speer when he was president of the schools, and Fry knew that she had worked closely with him. He testified that "she gave several emphatic reasons as to why, to the best of her belief, Elliott could not have written such a letter."

The subjects covered in the rest of Fry's testimony—dealing with Elder's stories about having the letters copied and Elder's complaints about his questioning, have been described earlier, except for two important details brought out by Bartlett at the end of Fry's questioning. First, Fry recalled a conversation he had had some years before with a former Mount Hermon teacher who had known Elder well. The teacher (who had died in 1932) had told Fry that he had had "a long talk with Tom Elder. He feels that he has never been adequately dealt with at Mount Hermon, that he would have been better off if he had accepted some positions that were offered him years ago." Second, Fry testified that it was well known that Elder had been considered for the position of headmaster of Mount Hermon before Speer was chosen in 1931. Elder had wanted the job badly. Another former teacher told Fry, "Oh, Elder's ambition was well known. In fact it was difficult for some of the teachers. He made it difficult."

With those suggestions of the dean's possible motives, Bartlett ended his questioning of Fry.

December 5, 1934

∽

Grandin and Bartlett

The first witness on this day appears to have been John Grandin, member of the board of trustees and of its executive committee. He provided some details that afforded some insight into Elder and his reaction to the trustees' decision not to name him acting headmaster in the aftermath of Elliott Speer's murder. Grandin described Elder's appearance when Elder came into the meeting of the executive committee: "he was very, very red . . . and when I shook hands with him his hand was very hot." Elder, of course, had already been told by Fry that a committee would be appointed—that Elder would not be running the school—and the dean had said to Fry that he would rather resign. Elder repeated that sentiment at the meeting, while grudgingly accepting the appointment to serve under Porter.

Concerning the Dear Tom letter, Grandin testified, "I am absolutely convinced that he [Speer] didn't write the letter." In part this was because the complimentary comments about Elder in the letter did not square with what Speer had told Grandin in a number of conversations about the dean. Bartlett asked Grandin whether he had ever known Speer to be deceptive. The straight-talking Grandin was unequivocal. "I have never known Elliott Speer to be anything but one of the straightest shooters I ever came in contact with."

Grandin also testified that he had read the letters many times and had come to feel that the same person had written both of them. Like many others who knew Speer and who had read the letters, he did not think Speer would have used the slang words "fire" or "bunk" in a letter. "I could imagine him using the word 'firing' or 'bunk,' as I might myself, but in sitting down to write a letter as Headmaster, that phraseology would be foreign to him because he had gentlemanly instincts and would not have used that language."

Grandin also recounted the events of October 17, when he had come to campus with his son. Grandin was instrumental during that visit in getting Elder to show the detectives where he had had the letters copied. By that time Grandin knew that Elder had been grilled by the detectives, and he told the dean that he was sorry he was having a tough time. But he went on to say, "If you would just clear up this matter of these letters, Mr. Elder, it would help us all. Then we could go along and run our school."

Elder was angry, and snapped, "I don't think the Trustees want to help clear up this matter." Grandin, surprised at Elder's reaction, responded, "That's a funny statement. I am here to do anything in the world to clear up these matters. I will give $5000 today to know who wrote those letters and where they were written." Elder then proposed that he and Grandin go "a reasonable distance to solve this matter." Not wanting to take on the investigation himself without the knowledge of the authorities, Grandin said he would get back to the dean. He then talked with the detectives, who said they would go with Elder if he was willing. Dasey and Grandin immediately drove down to Elder's house and said they were ready to go. Dasey said to Elder, "Put your cards on the table, where do you want us to go, Mr. Elder, and why do you want us to go?" Elder said, "I want you to go to Springfield." It was decided that Elder and his lawyer and Dasey would go. (More on this trip to Springfield is given in later testimony.)

Following Grandin's testimony, Bartlett himself took the stand. Then, as now, it is unusual for the prosecuting attorney to testify. In this case, however, Bartlett had been involved from the beginning as an investigator and there were some events that only he could testify about. In particular, he recounted to Judge Hayes his conversations with Elder about the letters. Bartlett was anxious to put on record the dean's inconsistent stories about the copying of the letters (as described in Chapter 5).

As already narrated, on September 28, just after he had received copies of the letters from Fry, Bartlett, without revealing that he knew of the letters, had asked Elder if there was any additional correspondence that the dean had not turned over to the detectives. Elder initially denied it, until Bartlett told him he had heard of some correspondence between Speer and the dean relating to people and policy in the school. Elder then had retreated a little and admitted that there were letters, but he maintained that they were "of a very confidential nature." Bartlett testified that he had insisted on seeing the letters and that ultimately he and Elder had driven to the latter's home, where Elder retrieved the copies of the letters and turned them over to him.

Bartlett testified that after he had pointed out to Elder that the Dear Tom letter was not signed, Elder had embarked on a series of often contradictory explanations as to which letters were copies, why copies had been made, and what had happened to the originals.

Bartlett then testified about another conversation with the dean. Elder related to Bartlett an exchange he claimed to have had with Elliott Speer. Elder said he had asked the headmaster whether he believed in the immortality of the soul. According to Elder, Speer told him, "Tom, I have no doubt of it." Elder told Bartlett he had replied to the headmaster, "Well, old man, I fear I haven't that much faith that I believe I will actually see my mother and father."

The next witness, the detective John Stokes of the Massachusetts State Police, recounted the questioning of Elder through the night and early morning of October 5 and 6, which has already been described.

December 6, 1934

᠄

Concerning the Gun, and Elder's Movements

The first witness on this day was Merwin D. Birdsall, Elliott Speer's friend, whom everyone called David. He testified that he had known Elliott since 1924. During the summer of 1934, he and his family had visited the Speer family on their island on Lake Timagami (leased from the Canadian government for $15 per year) and had helped them build their small cabin there.

He told the judge that he had received a telephone call from Mr. Welles, Holly's father, about 8:30 on the night of September 14 and had immediately driven over to Ford Cottage, a short distance from his house on campus. He saw no other cars except the maid's.

There was little that was new in his testimony, except for his description of a visit from Dean Elder to his house on September 29. At that time, Elder asked Birdsall whether he had ever heard Elliott Speer express any unfriendly feeling toward him. Birdsall said no. Elder explained that there was a letter in the files that was bothering him, or that could not be explained—Birdsall could not remember Elder's exact words.

Asked about the Speer family, Birdsall said, "It would be hard to find a family that was more congenial or enjoyed life more than they did."

As he left the stand, Birdsall (who had previously worked as a cashier at the local bank) suggested to the judge that Elder's bank account should be examined for any unusual withdrawals. Bartlett asked, "You have in mind the possibility of purchase or hiring somebody to do it?" Birdsall said yes. Bartlett told him, and the judge, that, "yes, that was done." Apparently, nothing unusual had been discovered.

Among the subsequent witnesses were Daniel Bodley and William Dierig, who repeated their recollection of hearing a shot on the evening of September 14 after seeing a dark sedan drive past them in the direction of Ford Cottage, and then, following the shot, of seeing the same car drive rapidly away from the area. Curiously, neither was asked whether the car had one headlight out.

Also, one Adam Wolfskiel, a local real estate broker and stringer for the *Boston Herald* in Greenfield, testified that on the morning after the shooting he found shotgun wadding about 20 feet west of the broken window at Ford Cottage. He gave the wadding to Captain Van Amburgh, the firearms expert who was there at the time.

Van Amburgh himself testified next. He explained that the shot had been fired through the study window on the northerly side of the headmaster's house. The shotgun slugs or pellets made a pattern in the screen with a diameter of about 4½ inches. There were eight distinct holes in the screen, one larger than the others, indicating that two slugs had gone through the same hole. Nine pellets, he told the judge, is the conventional load for certain sizes of shot in a 12-gauge shotgun. According to Van Amburgh, the wadding that Mr. Wolfskiel found was the size of 12-gauge wadding. The medical examiner had given Van Amburgh the pellets recovered from Elliott Speer's body, and he had also obtained the pellets recovered from the headmaster's study. Their weight was consistent with double-o buckshot. From the height of the window and the location of the hole in the screen, Van Amburgh estimated that the angle of the muzzle must have been upward about five degrees and that the muzzle would have been about 15 feet from the screen when the shot was fired. Based on the size and uniformity of the pattern in the screen, he concluded that the gun had been fitted with a choke barrel, which reduces the bore, or diameter, of the muzzle.

On this day, also, the Speers' servants testified. Florence George testified that, after hearing the shot, she heard footsteps running away, "quick running steps" toward the north and east— that is, toward West Hall or Cottage Row or the driveway. Neither Constantine George, Florence's husband, who was not at Ford Cottage at the time of the shooting, nor Steffie Wozniak, the cook, had anything of relevance to offer, except Steffie did testify that she had never heard the Speers argue.

Bartlett then began presenting testimony relating to Dean Elder's movements on the night of the murder. A senior at Mount Hermon, Albert Larue, was Bartlett's next witness. Larue testified that he had visited the Elder household on the night of September 14. He said he had left his room on the third floor of Crossley and walked, by a roundabout route, to the Elders' house. He had started at 7:30 (he heard the Memorial Chapel clock strike once) and arrived about 8:00. (He had timed the walk since, and, he said, it took him 29½ minutes.) When he arrived, the Elders were folding up some mailings for Dean Elder's campaign for county commissioner. Larue testified that Elder left the house about 8:20, and he did not see the dean again before he left the house at 9:00. The night had been dark and foggy, he said.

Crucial testimony relating to Elder's whereabouts after 8:20 followed. Herman Miner, a mechanic at Morgan's Garage in East Northfield, testified that he had been on duty the evening of September 14 when Elder drove in. Miner was not sure about the time, but he said it was after 8:00, probably about 8:30. Elder's Buick had a headlight bulb out and Miner replaced it. Trying to fix the time, Miner recalled that a Mr. Hatch from Mount Hermon came into the garage 5 to 15 minutes after Elder left.

Attempting to tie down these time estimates, Bartlett called Miles E. Morgan, the owner of the garage, who testified that Mr. Hatch came into the garage about 8:45. Finally, William Alexander Mitchell, apparently an East Northfield resident, said he was working on his truck at Morgan's Garage on that night, and had arrived about 7:30. He testified that he had seen Elder come in about a half an hour later, and Hatch came in about fifteen minutes after Elder left. On this unsatisfactory note—full of "abouts" and "approximatelys"—the week's testimony ended.

December 10, 1934

∾

Francis Bayley

The next day of testimony began with the head of Mount Hermon's English Department, Louis Smith, whose lengthy testimony added very little to the sum of Judge Hayes's knowledge. Smith told the judge he was in Holbrook Hall on the evening of September 14, but he did not remember what time Dean Elder came in—it could have been anytime between 7:45 and 8:50. He did recall seeing a trooper come into the building at some point and ask one of the boys whether Mr. Speer was in the building. Elder was in the building at that time, and Smith had thought that Elder had not seen the trooper. He asked Elder, "Tom, did you see who that was?" Elder said, "Yes." But, Smith testified, "he seemed to have something on his mind."

Smith was shown the Dear Tom letter and commented, "I am very much interested in two things, the use of the word 'fire' and the use of the word 'bunk' which Mr. Speer used repeatedly in his conversation but I never saw it in writing."

Next to take the stand was Francis Bayley, a young math teacher. He also was in Holbrook Hall on the night of the shooting. When the trooper came in, he had asked Bayley, "Where is Mr. Speer?" Bayley had told him, "I don't know." He testified that he may have added, "I believe he is most likely up at his home." Then Bayley turned to Elder and said, "Tom, where is Elliott?" Elder said, "I don't know. I suppose up to his home. I'll find out." Elder picked up his phone to call Ford Cottage, but the trooper had already left.

Bayley testified that he listened while Elder spoke to someone at Ford Cottage. Bayley recalled that Elder seemed to be having trouble getting an answer to his question, "Is Mr. Speer there?" When Elder hung up the phone, he started out of his office. Bayley continued: "If I might say, he seemed to be greatly excited, and started to walk out. He said, 'Come with me,' and put his finger to his lips and motioned indicating the other people there, that he did not want them to know where we were going, and we walked out of the building." When they got outside, Elder told Bayley, "Something has happened to Elliott Speer." They drove up to Ford Cottage in Elder's car. Elder did not tell Bayley that Speer had been shot, so Bayley was completely unprepared when they walked into Ford Cottage and saw the headmaster lying in the hall, in a large pool of blood. After seeing Speer and the blood, Bayley said he had turned and walked back out the front door and then stood in the vestibule with David Birdsall. Birdsall said to him, "Isn't it a dreadful thing that he was shot?" Bayley said, "Do you mean suicide?" "No, no, not suicide," Birdsall told him. "He was shot."

Bayley was not strong on issues of time. He did not notice what time it was when he and Elder left Holbrook Hall, nor could he recall what time Elder had arrived there. He had earlier told investigators that Elder had come in between 7:50 and 8:10 that evening. In his inquest testimony, though, he said that that may have been an error—he heard someone come in but could not say whether it was Elder. In fact, he said, the time might have been nearer to 9:00 than to 8:00.

Bayley did provide some information that tended to explain another bit of evidence that had seemed important. A number of people, beginning with Wilfred Fry, had recalled that Dean Elder had a bandage on one of his hands when they saw him the day after the shooting. Bayley testified that when he and Elder arrived at Ford Cottage, they parked on the north side—opposite the window through which Speer had been shot—and the dean tripped going through the hedge and fell on his hands. Later, when Bayley saw the bandage on the dean's right hand, he asked Elder if he had hurt it when he tripped. Elder said yes.

Another teacher, Stephen Stark, head of the Mount Hermon Language Department, followed Bayley to the witness stand. Bartlett asked him to recount a conversation he had with Elder shortly after suspicion had begun to point to the dean. Stark recalled that Elder had called him into his office. Elder asked him, "You have heard rumors about these letters?" Stark had said, "Yes, in a general way. My knowledge is very slight, but I have heard the rumors that people around here are mentioning." The dean said, "Well, it's just that I want to speak about. I want you to understand that the letter which I presented to the Trustees was an actual, a faithful, an absolute copy of what Elliott Speer wrote to me in his own hand." Stark testified that he had replied noncommittally. Elder went on, "I want to tell you this also, that there were certain parts of that letter which were omitted by me when I had the copy made, and therefore it is not a perfect copy, but whatever was handed in was absolutely correct, but I omitted certain parts."

At this point, Bartlett asked Stark to read both the Dear Tom letter and the letter from Elder to Speer. Stark commented that the use of the word "confidential" in the beginning of the Dear Tom letter is "highly characteristic" of Elder, but not of Elliott Speer. The same is true, he said, of the phrase "not because we agree on all things." On comparing the two letters, he testified that he felt they "are more similar than two letters, written by two men so absolutely unlike as those two men are, would naturally be."

December 11, 1934

∽

More on the Gun, and King Watson

Another person who was working in Holbrook Hall on the night of the shooting, William Wilson, opened the day's testimony. He was a Mount Hermon graduate who had been working for the dean. He, like everyone else who testified on the subject, was unable to recall what time Dean Elder came into the building that night. He did say, however, that after Elder had been questioned by Bartlett, Elder asked Wilson if he knew what time Elder had come into the office. Wilson said he did not, and he testified that the dean had told him that, "as he remembered he had come in somewhere around ten minutes to eight, and I told him I still didn't remember anything about it."

Wilson was asked whether he was familiar with the late head-master's handwriting. He echoed others when he described it as practically illegible. He rarely received anything from Speer in his handwriting, and when he did, "it would be a very brief note, and I could never read it."

The next two witnesses, Daniel Van Valkenburgh father and son, were crucial to Bartlett's attempt to show that Elder was the killer. Elder had consistently denied owning a 12-gauge shotgun while at Mount Hermon. Daniel H., the son of Daniel Van Valken-burgh, was a constable in Gill, the tiny township in which the Mount Hermon campus is located, and a handyman employed at the school. He testified that about nineteen years earlier he had gone hunting with Elder, who had carried a 12-gauge, double-barreled, hammer shotgun with a very light-colored stock. Elder had told him that he had used the gun hunting turkeys down south and was not sure how it would handle buckshot. The witness went on that they had found that the gun could handle buckshot, but it "kicked like the dickens." He also recalled that the trigger guard on the gun was small, so that if you used two fingers to fire it, you would injure your fingers. Van Valkenburgh acknowledged that he had previously told police that he was not sure that Elder's gun on that occasion was a 12 gauge. But that was in Elder's presence, the witness said. Since then, he had become convinced that Elder was lying when he denied owning any gun other than the 20-gauge shotgun he had turned over to the police. So, Van Valkenburgh said, he was not reluctant to say under oath that he remembered very well that the gun Elder carried on that hunting trip was a 12-gauge shotgun.

Van Valkenburgh's father, the school's blacksmith—short and bent, with a white beard stained with tobacco—testified next and supported his son's testimony, saying that he, too, had hunted with Elder sometime between 1915 and 1920, and that Elder had used a 12-gauge shotgun at that time.

The inquest's afternoon session began with the testimony of David Porter, then chairman of the school's committee on administration, which had undertaken the headmaster's duties after September 14. He was asked only to recount the meeting at which the committee was appointed, recalling that Elder had asked the trustees to allow him to retire but had ultimately agreed to serve.

Porter, a relative newcomer to the school, was followed by the old-timer Richard L. Watson, the superintendent of buildings at the school, from which he had graduated in 1891. A very engaging witness, Watson was knowledgeable and plainly honest. The students called him "King" Watson, and they liked him. He habitually wore a red tie—which reflected his peppery temperament—and the senior class presented him with a new one each year. He testified that he had worked for Mount Hermon for forty-eight years (including his time as a student). He said he had known Thomas Elder for thirty of those years. Although he had seen Elder hunting, he could not say whether he was carrying a 12-gauge shotgun, since, he admitted, he would not know one gun from another.

When he had first read the Dear Tom letter, Watson said, he had felt that Elliott Speer had not written it. Bartlett made the obvious point: "The letter would never have been of any use [to Elder] while Mr. Speer was alive, would it?" Watson: "Never in the wide, wide world." Watson testified that Houghton, the detective introduced by Fry, had discussed the letters with him and had asked him to convince Elder to reveal where the letters had been copied. During a subsequent drive together, Watson said that Elder told him that he thought that one of the copies had been made in Springfield and the other in Boston. Elder had then called Bartlett with this news. Later, Watson went with Elder to Boston, to the Hotel Bellevue where Elder said he had stayed, and then to the Parker House, where Elder pointed out the stenographer to whom he said he had dictated one of the letters. She did not recall the incident. The next day, Elder told Watson he had gone to Springfield and had located the other stenographer, and that she had remembered him. Presumably this was the occasion when Elder had taken Dasey and his own lawyer with him.

As he had with some other witnesses, the judge asked Watson whether Elder had ever talked with him about immortality, or, as the judge put it, did he have "any conversation with you as to the next place, if any, the human soul is going to after it departs from this world?" Watson answered, "Tom was a man of faith, and since this thing has come up he has said that he has lost his faith in God, if that's what you mean." Asked directly if he thought Dean Elder could have killed Speer, Watson said, "I do not think he would have taken the chance."

(A few days before he testified, Watson was quoted in the *New York Journal* as saying: "If he did this terrible thing, and I can't possibly believe that he did, he is the greatest actor in the world. On the night of the murder he appeared more shocked and horrified than anyone. He seemed stupefied by the tragedy." He had continued, "You really can never believe this awful accusation. Of course I realize that there are some things like the letter which did seem peculiar. Then I do know he has always been terribly ambitious and that there was some talk about a girl.")

On leaving the stand, Watson, who had spent most of his life at Mount Hermon, turned to the judge and declared, "I love that old school, sir."

December 12, 1934

∽

Miscellaneous Witnesses

Gordon McEwan, the assistant treasurer of the schools, testified first. Bartlett was anxious to prove that Speer's purported promises to Elder in the Dear Tom letter were incredible. Referring to the annual retirement allowance of $3,000 promised in the letter, he asked McEwan, "Would he [Speer] have been likely to have taken up with you any such proposition?" "Most assuredly," said McEwan. He said that Mr. Speer was always careful to check with the budget committee before giving raises. Bartlett pointed out that the Dear Tom letter promised to raise Elder's salary to $4,000. McEwan: "When was that statement made?" Bartlett: "According to Mr. Elder that was made February 19, 1934." McEwan: "The budget committee meeting was held on April 30 when Mr. Elder's salary was submitted and the regular additions, [totaling] $3300."

Judge Hayes got the point. To hammer it home, Hayes asked McEwan, "Now for Mr. Speer to have said or written a letter to a person individually, saying that he would increase a man that much money, unless he had first taken it up with you or the [Budget] Committee, would be an unheard-of proposition. Is that what you mean?" McEwan: "Yes, sir."

After reviewing the Dear Tom letter, McEwan told Judge Hayes that he felt that Mr. Speer would not have written the words "there is not a single phase of the work that you cannot handle" to Dean Elder.

The school doctor, Bretney Miller, was next on the stand. A few days after the shooting, he testified, the dean showed him his right hand, which he said he had injured, and told Miller that he was afraid it might turn into "my old trouble of eczema returning." Several weeks later, Elder came to see the doctor in the infirmary. He tried to get Miller to recall the date of their previous conversation. Bartlett may have been suggesting that Elder was trying to get Miller to say that he saw the hand injury before the shooting, but the doctor's testimony did not support this.

Bartlett did, however, make some points through this witness.

Dr. Miller recalled Speer telling him in July of that year, "I have been kicking myself in the pants ever since school was out, that I didn't have foresight enough to give Mr. Elder a sabbatical year and leave of absence last spring when it should have been done and could have been [because of the dean's poor health], and now it can't be done."

Dr. Miller also felt strongly that the Dear Tom letter was not genuine. Bartlett asked, "You don't have any idea in the world that Elliott ever wrote that letter, do you?" Miller said, "It's not conceivable. Not in the wildest reach of my imagination do I think so."

Lester P. White, the Mount Hermon chaplain, formerly head of the Bible Department, followed the doctor. Reverend White had presided at the memorial service at Ford Cottage on the Sunday after the shooting. He testified to a conversation with Elliott Speer in November 1933. White testified that he had already known, from earlier conversations, that Speer was experiencing increasing difficulty in getting along with the dean. In the November conversation with White, Speer

> said that he had decided to bring some of the younger faculty into the office to help him [Elder] and work a little more congenially with him; that he knew that Tom would feel badly about it, and he did. He also told me on that occasion that Mr. Elder had been talking with him about the matter of a pension in case Mr. Elder should ever retire and Mr. Elder seemed to feel he should be entitled to a pension much larger than one would normally expect in his position and for his length of service, and Mr. Elder felt very strongly about it, and Elliott felt equally strongly about it [that is, disagreeing with Elder], which was the normal relationship between those two.

Reverend White had a view of the Dear Tom letter that was very thoughtful and differed from the opinions expressed by most of the witnesses who testified at the inquest. He said that, in his opinion, "parts of that letter are entirely expressions from letters which Elliott did write or they are recollections of conversations which Elliott may have had with Mr. Elder. I feel parts of the letter are genuine." But, when Bartlett asked him about the sentence

"There is not a single phase of the work that you cannot handle as well as I," White answered, "That is nonsense, I think, just plain nonsense."

The order of the remaining witnesses is not clear. The following is an attempted reconstruction. The order of witnesses, at any rate, is not crucial.

Patrolman Richard Hiller's testimony cleared up two small mysteries that the previous testimony had created. Hiller said that David Birdsall had called the Shelburne Falls barracks, where he was assigned, at 8:48 P.M. on September 14. In this call, Birdsall had reported that Elliott Speer had been shot, "foul play and very serious." Hiller and two other patrolmen left the barracks at 8:55 and reached Holbrook Hall, about fifteen miles away, between 9:15 and 9:20. Hiller knew the campus from previous calls and patrols, and he knew that Speer had an office in Holbrook Hall. He went into the building and asked whether Speer was there. He testified that he did not wait for an answer, because he could see that everything was serene there, and he concluded that the shooting must have been at the headmaster's residence. Arriving at Ford Cottage, Hiller observed Elliott Speer's body in the hall, with Mrs. Speer and Mrs. Birdsall sitting on the steps leading to the second floor. The patrolmen, guided by David Birdsall, went into the study and saw the broken window and the trail of blood from the headmaster's desk to the hallway. They immediately began a search outside, using the floodlights attached to their patrol car.

Hiller testified that later that night he had driven with Elder down to the latter's house (this must have been in connection with the investigators' attempt to examine all the guns on campus). He saw Elder take a 20-gauge shotgun out of his closet. He also noticed that the dean had a handkerchief on his hand, which was bleeding.

Hiller's evidence answered the small question of why troopers showed up at Holbrook Hall on the night of September 14. His asking for Speer in that building also supports Bayley's earlier testimony and tends to explain why the dean had called Ford Cottage and asked to speak to Speer.

Following Hiller to the witness stand was the undertaker,

George Kidder. Mr. Kidder, who prepared Elliott Speer's body for burial, opined, from the headmaster's wounds, that he had been standing, perhaps reaching for a book, when he was shot.

Louise Lovell, who was Elliott Speer's secretary, testified that she had never seen either of the February letters.

December 13, 1934

∾

More on Elder's Gun

(*None of the volumes* of the inquest transcript bear this date, but one of the undated volumes contains the testimony summarized below. It seems likely that this testimony followed that described above.)

Lee Anson Howard and his father provided testimony supporting Bartlett's contention—and the Van Valkenburghs' testimony—that Dean Elder had owned a 12-gauge shotgun. Lee Howard worked as an engineer at the Northfield Seminary's powerhouse. He had known Elder for about twenty years. He testified that when Elder went off to attend Cornell, he left a 12-gauge shotgun at Howard's father's house. During that time, his father had loaned it to someone who broke the stock, and a new stock was made for it. According to Howard, the replacement stock was maple and had never been stained, so it was very light in color. All this was before the war (meaning, of course, the First World War). The witness said that he believed that the gun had been returned to Elder.

Lee Howard's father, Anson, a plumber at the schools since 1890, testified to the same story, with a few more details. He recalled that Elder had retrieved the gun on his return from Cornell. He also remembered seeing the dean shooting clay pigeons "a good long time ago."

The next witness was Gordon Pyper, a young science teacher. He testified that Speer had asked him to help out Elder in the office during the summer. (This apparently was part of Elliott Speer's plan to bring younger men to work in the office with Elder, which he had described to Lester P. White.) After the murder,

Elder told Pyper his help was no longer needed. Later, Pyper heard that Speer had told someone that "he had an awful time convincing Tom Elder that Pyper should be in the office." But apparently there was no ill will between the families, for Pyper testified that just before Elder began his leave of absence, he brought his wife over to visit Mrs. Pyper. Elder stopped to talk with Pyper, who was working in his garden. The dean told him, "As for those damnable lies that are being spread about me, don't believe anything that is being said. I know that whatever happens to me, my wife will be 100 per cent for me." That prediction proved to be perfectly accurate.

December 14, 1934

෴

Mrs. Elder and the Dean

The last day of testimony began, coincidentally, with Grace Elder, the dean's wife, taking the stand. She had married Thomas Elder in 1911, she said, after he returned from Cornell. She also testified that she had seen a handwritten letter (probably referring to the February Dear Tom letter) the previous winter, from Speer to her husband. She testified that she had recognized Speer's handwriting. She described the letter and recalled that in it the headmaster had written that he would rather have Elder than any three heads of departments, and had discussed teachers and the dean's salary. In fact, she said she had seen both letters—the Dear Tom letter and the letter from Elder to Speer—both in longhand. "I should say Mr. Elder's was written in pencil probably and Elliott's was written in ink." She went on to say that Speer's letter contained "some things said about Dr. Cutler which we wouldn't care to keep." Asked where the originals were, she testified, "I suppose they were destroyed. There was no point in keeping them after the copies were made."

On other subjects, she was equally helpful to her husband. Did he have a 12-gauge shotgun? Not since "I have known him." When did the dean hurt his hand? When he went up to the Speers' house after the shooting.

Mrs. Elder did differ somewhat from her husband's story when she told the judge that Mr. Elder had left the house about 7:00 or 7:15 on the night of September 14, shortly after the Larue boy arrived. Mr. Elder had told her, she testified, that he was going to get the headlight on his car fixed.

Testing her, Bartlett asked how she happened to be familiar with the headmaster's handwriting. She said that her husband had received a long handwritten letter from Speer over the summer, when the Speer family was in Canada. (This, of course, would have been months after she could have seen the original, handwritten Dear Tom letter—which was dated in February—if there was one.)

Bartlett's next witness, Robert Bruce, a houseboy working at the Northfield Inn, provided some slight support for the contention that Elder owned a 12-gauge shotgun. This witness claimed to have seen an old 12-gauge shotgun in Elder's closet when he was employed by the dean to rake leaves the previous spring. He had not mentioned this to the detectives when he had first been questioned, he admitted, but claimed to have remembered it later. The strength of his evidence was not bolstered when he said he thought the stock of the gun had been dark.

Albert Roberts, the president of the Alumni Association and executive secretary of the schools, was the next witness. He testified that Speer had told him what he thought of Elder: "that Mr. Elder was a good man, that he had rendered good service to the schools across the years, but that he would like, in the particular position which he, Mr. Elder, occupied, to have somebody who was more in harmony with the modern idea of operating the schools. He would like to find some other position into which he could move Mr. Elder without hurting him."

Roberts said he had a conversation with Elder two or three weeks after the shooting. Elder had said to him, "You know, of course, that I didn't do this thing. How could I do it?" Elder had also said he had been charged with trumping up the Dear Tom letter. He said, "These letters are letters which I wrote and that Elliott wrote." Roberts's reply was that, having some knowledge of what the letters contained, he could not make that make sense.

Elder told him, "Nevertheless Elliott wrote every word of that letter."

Albert Dasey, the detective from the Massachusetts State Police, testified next. Unfortunately for our purposes, his testimony consisted largely of reading from the transcript of the questioning of Elder on October 20 and 21. That transcript is not duplicated in the inquest transcript, and it has not been located. Dasey did, however, also testify that there was a report by an expert named Osborne to the effect that the Dear Tom letter had indeed been typed by the stenographer identified by Elder. (This expert was either Albert S. Osborne or his son, Albert D. Osborne. Both later testified in the trial of Bruno Richard Hauptmann for the kidnapping and murder of the son of Charles and Anne Morrow Lindbergh.)

The dean's attorney, Charles Fairhurst, preceded his client on the stand. He turned over to the court (with his client's permission) a handwritten letter from Speer to Dean Elder. This was evidently the letter Mrs. Elder referred to as having been written during the summer from Canada.

The final witness was the dean himself. He had previously testified in the inquest only to identify his house on the map of the Mount Hermon campus. His testimony on this last day was more substantive, but anticlimactic. Speaking in his unique style, which combined a southern accent from his youth in Virginia with the clipped enunciation characteristic of Yankee speech, he calmly repeated the story he had told so many times. He was examined primarily by Judge Hayes (rather than Bartlett), and Hayes's questions basically consisted of assertions about the facts that might implicate the dean, which Elder was then given a chance to answer. It was not a probing cross-examination. So the dean's testimony consisted primarily of denials: No, he had not seen the book *The Public School Murder*; no, he had never owned a 12-gauge shotgun at Mount Hermon; no, he did not recall hunting with Van Valkenburgh. He acknowledged that he had engaged the services of Mr. Fairhurst the night after he was questioned by Houghton (whose real identity the dean still did not know). He admitted, "I think in all probability after I was questioned by the man

[Houghton] who came up with Mr. Bartlett that quite a little correspondence was destroyed." Judge Hayes asked, "Can you tell us what the letters referred to that you destroyed?" Dean Elder: "No. They were purely personal."

With respect to his movements on the night of September 14, the dean testified that he would have driven to Morgan's Garage in eight or ten minutes from his house, and that he thought he had returned to Holbrook Hall before 8:00 that evening.

Finally, he testified that he had shown the typewritten copies of the letters to Elliott Speer.

With that, the evidence-taking stage of the inquest came to an end. It only remained for Judge Hayes to decide whether there was sufficient evidence to send the case against the dean to a grand jury.

January 9, 1935

∽

Judge Hayes's Report

After studying the evidence for several weeks, Judge Hayes issued his report. He found that the evidence failed to "prove that any suspect was at the scene of the murder at the time it was committed." He acknowledged that there was circumstantial evidence against a suspect, whom he did not identify, but he said that the evidence was not strong. In the report he wrote: "From the evidence at the inquest some facts are made certain, namely that there were no eyewitnesses to the shooting, that the shot was fired from a .12-gauge shotgun; that this gun has never been discovered." He continued that there was no "believable evidence that any suspect was the owner of a 12-gauge shotgun within a period of about 19 years prior to this murder." With respect to the evidence of the Dierigs and Bodleys about the automobile, he wrote that "the night was dark and none of these four witnesses could say who was in the automobile, whether it was being driven by a man or woman, whether it contained one person or several or whether the number plate bore the color of 1934 Massachusetts number plates." There was no mention in Judge Hayes's findings of the Dear Tom and Dear Elliott letters.

The judge also declared that the evidence had shown that Elliott Speer had been on the best of terms with the faculty, students, and employees of the school and had lived in a harmonious household.

He concluded that the murder of Elliott Speer had been committed by "a person unknown to me."

8

Was Judge Hayes Right?

❧..❧

Judge Hayes's decision, predictably, did not satisfy many people. Some blamed the investigators. On January 10, 1935, the *Greenfield Recorder Gazette* editorialized, praising the local authorities but criticizing the state investigators: "As long as the investigation was conducted by men regularly assigned to this territory, matters were conducted cleanly and fairly. As soon as Stokes and his fellows from a distance appeared, there began one of the most intensive and irresponsible campaigns of villification (*sic*) and inuendo (*sic*) we have ever witnessed." The editorial concluded that "in the present head of the state detective force [Stokes] this newspaper finds a man seemingly more actuated by political ambition than sense of decency and for whom it can have little respect."

The editors of the *Lawrence (Mass.) Telegram* took a similar view: "Apparently they muffed something. Those who expected the arrest of the murderer were disappointed and those who did not expect an arrest after so much noise and little real sleuthing were vindicated in their opinion. Most of the sleuthing was apparently done in the newspapers. Everyone connected with the investigation camped on the front pages and got their pictures published, but that is about all. Naturally it is a puzzling case, but not one that requires so much publicity during the supposed secret work of running down the offender." Neither newspaper, of course, was privy to the evidence that had been presented at the inquest.

The newspapers' views aside, we should ask: Was Judge Hayes correct? And can we, from the distance of many decades, with all the witnesses dead, come to a reasoned conclusion about the decision?

Some of the inquest testimony cannot be located (about ninety pages of the transcript, out of more than twelve hundred, are missing), and we cannot recapture the visual clues that jurors and judges use to decide whether a witness is truthful or deceitful. Nevertheless, we can analyze what we have and see if we agree or disagree with Judge Hayes. Since the target of the inquest was obviously Dean Elder, we will focus on the evidence as it implicates or vindicates him.

Evidence of Motive

The evidence, which is not very full on the subject of the dean's possible motives, suggests two possible reasons that Elder might have wanted Elliott Speer killed. First, the dean was ambitious. He had wanted, even expected, to be named headmaster and had been disappointed when Elliott Speer had been chosen to replace Dr. Cutler. Wilfred Fry testified that Elder had been considered for the position (presumably in 1931) and that the dean had sought the job of acting headmaster as soon as Fry arrived after the shooting. Fry also described Elder's extreme frustration, even anger, at being asked merely to serve on a committee (not even as chairman) that would perform the duties of the headmaster. Fry also quoted a former teacher at Mount Hermon who had told him that Elder's "ambition was well known." John Grandin's testimony also described Elder's very emotional state at the September 16 meeting in which he was asked to serve on that committee. All of this demonstrates Elder's ambition and the depth of his disappointment in not being named headmaster.

The other motive, perhaps tied in with ambition, could have been fear. Certainly Grandin, Fry, Roberts, and, no doubt, many others knew that Elliott Speer would have liked to retire Elder and found it difficult to work with him. It is hard to believe that Elder did not also know this, either from Speer himself, or from the general talk and gossip common in small communities. Although Speer had been counseled to go slowly on this issue, he had been headmaster for two years in September 1934, and he may have felt that he was now free to take action. It is not inconceivable that he and Elder had spoken about this. Speer and Elder had been talking about pensions in late 1933, according to the testimony of the chaplain, Lester White, and the two men had apparently differed sharply about the size of the pension to which Elder should be entitled. Certainly Elder had reason to fear that Speer might very well find a way to end his career.

Finally, Elder had expressed bitterness about the way he had been treated by the school, according to Fry. Could the combination of this anger, ambition, and fear have turned the dean into a killer?

The Dear Tom Letter

ༀ

Proof that someone had a motive to kill the murder victim does not prove that he did the killing. (Indeed, it is a staple of mystery fiction that a large number of the characters have strong motives to kill the victim.) The Dear Tom letter, if it was in fact forged by the dean, likewise does not prove that the dean was a killer, only that he was a forger. But the forging and use of the letter by the dean, if that is what happened, are evidence of motive and even some evidence of at least a plan to do away with Elliott Speer. Bartlett had asked Richard Watson, "The letter would never have been of any use while Mr. Speer was alive, would it?" Watson: "Never in the wide, wide world."

Every witness who expressed an opinion about the Dear Tom letter—excepting only Dean Elder and his wife—testified that at least portions of it could not have been written by Elliott Speer.

Holly Speer's testimony, given after she saw the letter for the first time while she was on the stand, is very persuasive, as is other testimony based on the letter's style and the contradictions between statements in the letter and Speer's known opinions and plans. For example, in the letter Speer supposedly wrote that he would be spending more time away from the school in the future and expected to rely on Elder to run the school in his absences "exactly as well as I." Mrs. Speer, Fry, and Grandin all agreed emphatically that Elliott was not planning to be away from Mount Hermon more often—just the opposite, in fact, and that he certainly did not think that Elder could run the school as well as he did.

Even more telling, though, is the testimony of Gordon McEwan, the assistant treasurer of the schools. He confirmed that at the April meeting of the budget committee Elder's salary was raised to $3,300, not the $4,000 purportedly promised in the February Dear Tom letter. Further, he testified that Speer would certainly have talked with him about any salary increase or retirement allowance such as those proposed in that letter. Norton, the cashier, testified that no one except the headmaster received fuel, electricity, and lawn care, contrary to the promises in the Dear Tom letter. Elder's assertion that these promises must have "slipped Elliott's mind" is, to say the least, unpersuasive. So too is his explanation for having only an unsigned copy of the Dear Tom letter. As Elliott Speer's father testified, "It's inconceivable . . . that the original letter could have been destroyed with the assurances that it contained, and that [Elder] could have been satisfied by substituting for it a typewritten copy of only a portion of it without any signature attached."

But even if we are convinced that Elder forged the Dear Tom letter, and that the letter would not have been of any value to him as long as Elliott Speer was alive, is that enough to convict him of the murder? Might his attorney raise a reasonable doubt, suggesting that even if the letter was not genuine, perhaps it represented an old man's fantasy of what he would like the headmaster to write, or even a proposal that he could suggest that the headmaster sign?

The Murder Weapon

The 12-gauge shotgun that was used to commit the murder has never been found. The lack of a murder weapon made Bartlett's task much more difficult. He managed to produce several witnesses who testified that they had seen Dean Elder with such a gun many years earlier. Both Daniel H. Van Valkenburgh and his father Daniel swore that they could recall the dean with a 12-gauge shotgun at least nineteen or twenty years before. The gun, they said, had a very light-colored stock and was able to handle buckshot. Another father-son team, Anson Howard and Lee Anson Howard (there seems to have been a shortage of first names in the area), supported this testimony, even recounting the story that the stock of the gun had been broken and then replaced with the light-colored maple stock. This evidence about the gun, though, was substantially weakened by the fact that Daniel H. Van Valkenburgh had initially told investigators that he was not sure that the dean's gun had been a 12-gauge. Additionally, none of these witnesses could recall seeing the gun, or Dean Elder using it, for many years. Bartlett attempted to strengthen this aspect of his case with Robert Bruce's testimony. This houseboy from the Northfield Inn testified that the previous spring, while helping the Elders clean up their yard after the spring floods, he glimpsed a 12-gauge shotgun in a closet in their house. At a trial, though, a cross-examiner would have forced the boy to admit that he had not mentioned this at all to investigators when first questioned and that, at any rate, his identification of the gun from this quick, partial glimpse might well be doubted. Bruce also testified that he thought the weapon had a dark stock. If so, the gun was probably not the one described by the other witnesses.

Bartlett also made an effort to connect the injury to Elder's hand, which Fry and many other witnesses noticed, to the shotgun. Van Valkenburgh, the son, testified that the 12-gauge shotgun that he had seen Elder use "kicked like the dickens" when it was loaded with buckshot and that the trigger guard was small—if you used two fingers to fire it, he said, you would injure your fingers.

The possible connection between this and Elder's injured hand, however, took a number of heavy blows. Mr. Bayley, the young math teacher who accompanied the dean to Ford Cottage on the night of September 14, recalled that Elder had tripped over the hedge when they arrived and that the dean had told him that was when he had hurt his hand. Bayley had not noticed any injury to the dean's hand before arriving at the headmaster's house. A number of other witnesses, including the school's doctor, testified that Elder's skin was very delicate and that he was always having trouble with it. In short, the injury to the dean's hand does not add to the likelihood that he was the killer.

So, while there is some evidence that the dean had owned and used a 12-gauge shotgun while at Mount Hermon, no one was able to testify that the dean had recently used such a weapon or, for that matter, that he had purchased ammunition for it. Judge Hayes was justified in finding no "believable evidence" that Dean Elder had owned a 12-gauge shotgun during the two decades prior to the shooting of the headmaster.

Time and Opportunity

Even more than the evidence about the dean's shotgun, the testimony about his whereabouts at the time of the shooting is frustrating and contradictory.

First, when did the shooting take place? The first news of the shooting reached the police at 8:48, when David Birdsall called the Shelburne Barracks, according to Richard Hiller, the first trooper to respond. Holly Speer testified that she heard the shot "after eight." Her father, Henry Welles, who had been reading in the drawing room near Elliott Speer's study, had looked at his watch "after Elliott had lain on the floor for a little while, and I calculated that it was about 8:20, or perhaps a few minutes prior to that that he had been shot." David Birdsall testified that he was called by Mr. Welles about 8:30. All in all, then, we can agree with Mr. Welles that the fatal shot was fired between 8:15 and 8:20.

Where does the evidence place Dean Elder at this time? He

testified that he had returned from Morgan's Garage and had arrived at Holbrook Hall at 7:40 or 7:45 and did not leave until after
he had called Ford Cottage and learned that Speer had been shot.
Mrs. Elder testified that her husband had left their house between
7:00 and 7:15, shortly after, she said, the Larue boy had arrived.
However, Albert Larue, the Mount Hermon senior, testified that
he left Crossley Hall on the way to the Elders' house about 7:30
and took a walk of almost exactly half an hour before arriving at
the house. He further went on to testify that Dean Elder left about
8:20.

Elder, of course, said that when he left his home he drove to
Morgan's Garage to get a headlight fixed. That drive, he said,
would take 8 to 10 minutes from his house. The mechanic who
fixed the light testified that Elder arrived at the garage sometime
after 8:00, probably 8:30. He remembered that a Mr. Hatch had
arrived at the garage 5 to 15 minutes after Elder had left. Mr. Morgan, the owner of the garage, testified that Hatch came to the
garage about 8:45. Another gentleman who was working on his
truck at the garage recalled that he had arrived about 7:30, that
Elder drove in 30 minutes to an hour later, and that Hatch did
indeed come to the garage about 15 minutes after Elder left. In
sum, these three witnesses have Elder arriving at the garage between 8:00 and 8:30 and leaving about 8:30 or a little after. This is
flatly inconsistent with both Dean Elder's and Mrs. Elder's testimony, but it is not necessarily contradicted by Larue's evidence
that Elder left his house about 8:20.

No one who testified at the inquest remembered seeing the
dean before the time of the shooting. In fact, no one recalled
seeing him arrive at Holbrook Hall that evening. But he was defi-
nitely there when Patrolman Hiller arrived after 9:00.

Could the dean have left his house, driven to Ford Cottage—a
matter of only a minute or two—parked his car near the residence,
walked over with a shotgun, fired through the study window, returned quickly to his car, and driven from there to Morgan's Garage, within the time consistent with this testimony? If we posit
that Larue's testimony is accurate (discounting the Elders' testimony, since it is contradicted by virtually every other witness), that

Elder left his house about 8:20 (say, 8:15), he could certainly have been at the headmaster's window by 8:20. If he fired the shot then, he could have driven to Morgan's Garage by 8:30 (a journey of only two and one-half miles) and then returned to Holbrook Hall well before 9:00. Here, the testimony of Daniel Bodley and William Dierig, that they saw a dark sedan drive up from the lower campus after 8:15, then heard a shot, and shortly after saw the sedan come back past them and head off campus, could support this reconstruction. Unfortunately, they could not identify the car—they thought maybe it was a Franklin, a few years old. Dean Elder's car was a Buick. Franklin and Buick sedans from the early 1930s, however, do look very similar.

If we accept this time line—the dean leaving his home about 8:15, arriving at Ford Cottage a few minutes later, almost immediately firing his 12-gauge shotgun through the study window, returning quickly to his car, and arriving at Morgan's Garage a little after 8:30—what about the weapon? Conceivably, he could have thrown the gun into the Connecticut River on his way to Morgan's Garage, or even found a place to hide it on his way back. It is even possible that he kept it in his car's trunk until he found a good hiding place. There is no evidence that the police searched the campus thoroughly for several days, and no evidence at all that they searched Elder's house or his car.

So, on the basis of the evidence that we have from the inquest transcripts, we can say that it is *conceivable* that Dean Elder was the murderer. He had a motive; he very likely forged a letter that would have been useful to him only if Elliott Speer was dead; he may have owned a 12-gauge shotgun; and he had time—barely—to fire the shot and arrive at Morgan's Garage by the time witnesses placed him there.

But is that enough to convict him of the crime beyond a reasonable doubt, or even enough to send the case to a grand jury? Against the guilt of Dean Elder, his attorney would argue that the murder weapon had not been found; there were no eyewitnesses; the dean had no criminal record, and no record of violence or threats of violence; the evidence that he had a 12-gauge shotgun at any time near September 1934 is very weak; there is no evidence, despite a massive investigation, that he purchased buckshot or any other ammunition; and, finally, the dean's precarious health would make it very unlikely he could have performed the killing in the manner and within the time limits set by the testimony. At least one doctor had told Bartlett that he thought Elder's heart condition would have prevented him from carrying out the crime. The testimony of such an expert witness might be enough, by itself, to establish a reasonable doubt.)

Moreover, other bits of evidence presented at the inquest turned out to be irrelevant. Elder denied that he had read *The Public School Murder,* the English detective novel that appeared to describe the killing, and no witness could contradict him. (And, even if he had read it, it is hard to see how that would be admissible as evidence of his guilt.) The fact that Elder was the first to call Ford Cottage after the shooting—which at first had seemed suspicious—was explained by Elder's understandable concern aroused by the appearance of a trooper at Holbrook Hall looking for Speer. Similarly, the injury to Elder's hand—also suspicious if not explained—cannot be connected to his use of a shotgun. Bayley testified that Elder had tripped on arrival at Ford Cottage and had fallen to his hands. No one had noticed the dean's hands bleeding or bandaged at Holbrook Hall before he left to go to Ford Cottage.

Lacking a murder weapon, or a history of violence, or eyewitnesses, Judge Hayes was probably right in refusing to allow the case to go further. (It is worth pointing out that District Attorney Bartlett's presentation of the evidence at the inquest was remarkably—and commendably—fair to the suspect, Dean Elder. He was scrupulous in revealing to Judge Hayes when witnesses had made prior statements to the police inconsistent with their testimony, and he was generous in allowing Dean Elder and his wife to state the dean's alibi.)

In a newsreel reporting on the beginning of the inquest, District Attorney Bartlett addressed the moviegoers: "We feel and hope that this inquest will be of considerable assistance in the solution of this case. But, in any event, everyone may rest assured that the Massachusetts authorities will not cease their efforts until a solution of this crime has been reached."

After Judge Hayes's report finding the evidence insufficient to charge anyone for the murder, Lieutenant Dasey nevertheless declared, according to an article in the *Boston Traveler* datelined January 10, that "the case is already solved" and that the authorities were continuing to search for additional evidence against the killer.

The authorities still believed that Elder was the killer—and, eventually, there was a major break in the case.

9

Watching the Dean, 1934—1937

❦❧

The police continued their investigation after the inquest. They tapped the telephone in Ford Cottage for a period, apparently until the Speer family moved out. The archives at the school contain many pages of pencil transcripts of calls to and from Ford Cottage. Presumably, this tap was made with the approval of Holly Speer. She was certainly not a suspect. The police were hoping to hear someone threaten the family or to catch some other clue to the identity of the killer.

The focus, though, was still on Elder. The police established a "mail cover"—every piece of mail sent to or from the Elder household in Alton, New Hampshire, was noted and a tracing made of the front of the envelope, including the address, return address, and postmark. This continued into 1937. The school archives contain literally hundreds of these tracings, as well as spreadsheets showing the identity of the correspondents and the dates of the letters. Apparently the letters were not routinely opened, although some may have been.

Seeking some connection between Elder and his former secretary, the police also traced Miss Dill's telephone calls for a period, and her mail, like that of the Elders, was checked.

Another amateur investigator entered the scene briefly. After the inquest (probably during the summer of 1935), the former headmaster, Dr. Henry Cutler, returned to see if he could solve the crime. He was using his retirement to study medicine at the Sorbonne in Paris. After arriving by ship in Philadelphia and meeting there with Fry, he traveled to Greenfield to meet with Bartlett (who was no longer the district attorney), who filled him in on the inquest and allowed him to read reports of witness interviews. Cutler then met with Elder in New Hampshire. He also spoke with Richard Watson and Elder's lawyer, Charles Fairhurst.

His report of the results of this investigation, in a handwritten letter on United States Lines stationery—presumably written on the voyage back to France—provides some fascinating insights, if the report is accurate. Cutler found Elder resolutely claiming innocence:

> Mr. Elder protested his innocence again and again. He said the letters were real and the copies were identical. [We cannot help but wonder if Elder told Cutler that he had omitted portions of the Dear Tom letter unflattering to Cutler.] He was of the opinion that notes were in existence to prove the truth of the statements contained in the letters. . . . He regretted his presentation of the letters at a time when all was centered on the tragedy. He told of the events of the Friday evening [September 14]—and where he was.

Equally predictable, Watson was still ambivalent: "Mr. W. related the details of the crime and of Mr. Elder's attitude and the letters and his experience with the officers and detectives. Mr. W. believes [in Elder's innocence] but sometimes doubts." Cutler's talk with Elder's attorney, Fairhurst, yielded an unsurprising assertion of Elder's innocence. It's likely that Bartlett (with the approval of the district attorney's office) gave Cutler access to the witness interview notes, and other access only partly because of Cutler's status as the highly respected elder statesman of Mount Hermon. He also expected, and received, a report from Cutler of his talks with Elder—Bartlett was hoping that Elder would confess or at least implicate himself when he spoke to his old mentor.

Interestingly, Cutler recounts his conversation with Bartlett, in his unique shorthand: "I saw Mr. Joseph Bartlett. I asked him who shot Elliott Speer. He ans. that is a pretty dirct quest. and I can not ans. it—but I can tell you who did not shoot Elliott Speer—Thomas E. Elder." This recollection, that Bartlett told him that he believed Elder to be innocent, is extremely unlikely. He may simply have misunderstood. Bartlett may have said that there was not enough evidence to convict Elder or that he may have come to believe that Elder was part of a conspiracy to kill Speer, but not the actual killer. A better clue to Bartlett's attitude toward the dean is contained in correspondence with William Houghton, the Secret Service agent who had briefly helped with the investigation. Shortly before the inquest, Bartlett wrote to Houghton and asked that he testify. Bartlett explained what he hoped would be the outcome of the inquest:

> The reason I would like you here is this. The more we get into this case the more we come to believe that Elder actually did the deed, or knows something very definite about it. I think the officers are all pretty much convinced that he is the one. He is extremely cautious himself and has a clever attorney. It is a safe guess that any evidence which would convict him has been carefully destroyed or concealed, therefore the only hope is for a break on his part. The officers believe, and I think justly, that were he arrested and kept in jail two or three days he might crack up nervously and tell the whole thing.

Cutler's biography by Richard Day, *A New England School-master, The Life of Henry Franklin Cutler* (which likely reflects Cutler's views, even though it was published after his death, since Mrs. Cutler was active in its preparation and owned the copyright), may more accurately describe and explain Cutler's final views about the crime. Dean Elder is described in the book as "a brilliant but unstable man" and "a disruptive and discordant influence." The author quotes from a letter Cutler wrote to one of the trustees after his visit to the former dean: "I think Mr. Elder knows more than anybody else. . . . I am sorry that I cannot report any more advancement in the solution of the terrible murder. I think the truth will be known. Up to the present, I must acknowledge, the clue that leads to Mr. Elder is the most plausible of all the clues." In Day's opinion, "the key to Cutler's interpretation of what he found, is that he refused to let himself even guess at Elder's guilt until it was proven."

The plan to use Cutler to trap Elder failed. In fact, it backfired. According to Lieutenant-Detective Maurice Nelligan, who attended (at Cutler's invitation) a meeting between Cutler and Elder,

> Nothing much of materiality developed at the interview. Tom Elder talked incessantly but did not say much, with the old Doctor listening and fondly gazing into Tom's face. The thought struck me that I was between a fine old gentleman in his dotage on one hand and an insane man on the other hand.
>
> Elder did a lot of talking as I said before, which indicated to me that Dr. Cutler would learn of some inconsistent statement of Tom's and would say to Tom, "Did you say that" and Tom would satisfy Dr. Cutler that he, Tom, was all right on the statement in question because he might have been mistaken as the tragedy happened a long time ago and it is difficult to remember because Van Valkenburgh was sore because his son was not allowed to continue at Mt. Hermon, that Larue was faulty and unreliable, that Roberts was not what he should be, that Miner at Morgan's garage was vindictive and a perjurer. Because of the foregoing I disliked to talk much with Dr. Cutler. He evidently tells all he knows to Elder. Elder found a lot of fault with everybody who differed with him, but in all our interview Elder never mentioned the Dear Tom and Dear Elliott letters which are really the nucleus of the whole case and he knows it.

Meanwhile, Elder was watched by detectives while he attended some public events. There is at least one surveillance report describing Elder's activities (all perfectly innocent) at a meeting of the Holstein Breeders Association in 1936.

Unfortunately, there is no mention of Elder's attendance at a meeting of the Holstein-Friesian Association in Keene, New Hampshire, in May 1937, which came to have quite a bit of significance.

10

"Norton, I want to talk to you"

❧❦

After the inquest, with its failure even to name a suspect, the case disappeared from public consciousness, at least outside of northern Massachusetts. But in May 1937, the mystery leapt back onto the front pages.

S. Allen Norton, retired treasurer of Mount Hermon School, excitedly called the police late on Tuesday, May 26, 1937, to claim that Thomas Elder, the retired dean, had threatened him with a gun. At about 11:00 P.M. he had returned from a meeting at the church with his wife and had left her at the front door of their home in Greenfield. He had opened the garage door to put his car in the garage when Elder appeared out of the darkness, wearing a long coat. Elder said, "Hey, Norton, I want to talk to you. Do as I say. I want to talk to you." Elder then, according to Norton, took a shotgun from under his coat and pointed it at him. Thoroughly frightened, Norton ducked behind his car and ran into the house. He called the police. They issued an alarm for Elder and finally arrested him the next morning at his home in Alton, New Hampshire.

Elder waived extradition and was brought to Greenfield to be arraigned. According to his attorney, Charles Fairhurst, the same man who had represented Elder at the inquest, Elder said he did not want to fight extradition because he "knew nothing about" the incident. Elder had an alibi. He said he had been attending a meeting of the Holstein-Friesian Association of America—an organization of cattle breeders, of which Elder was a director—in Keene, New Hampshire, on May 26 and had spent the night with his wife at the Eagle Hotel in that city, some forty miles north of Greenfield. Once again stolidly behind her husband, Mrs. Elder told reporters, "I was with my husband all the time, so I know. Of course there is no truth to what we have heard. The people here have been very nice to us and we are both extremely sorry that such a matter should arise when we were so happy in Alton." Fairhurst told the press that Mr. and Mrs. Elder had retired early to bed in the hotel—about 7:30 or 8:00 on the evening of the 26th—and had risen about 7:00 in the morning for breakfast before driving home to Alton.

The police, on the other hand, were most anxious to convict Elder on these charges. They had already found a witness. Yvonne Arsenault, the maid for one of Norton's neighbors, told police that she had seen a man wearing a long coat approach Norton and later run down the driveway. She said he was carrying a gun and drove off. The car she described, police said, resembled Elder's.

The newspapers, whose reporters remembered that Elder had been the chief suspect in the Speer case three years earlier, were quick to suggest a connection with the Speer murder. On its front page, the *New York Times* headlines described Elder as an "Aide to Slain Dr. Speer" and an "Important Figure in Unsolved Murder." The accompanying story recounted Elliott Speer's murder and the subsequent investigation. It noted, pointedly, that the authorities at the time had said that the investigation into the killing had "centered 'close to the Speer household.'" The article continued, "Every worthwhile clue turned the investigators back toward the Mount Hermon campus."

This connection was made even more directly the next day. According to the *Times,* Norton had been giving police information relating to the headmaster's killing. State detectives, the paper reported, had disclosed that, in a series of interviews continuing up to a week before the assault, Norton had given them "new and vital information about the unsolved murder." The assistant district attorney, at the arraignment, told the court, "Not only is this a serious crime, but there is also a possibility that it has a background of a much more serious crime."

According to newspaper reports, the information that Norton provided was considered so important that the Massachusetts State Police sent investigators to Greenfield to meet with Norton. In order not to alert the locals that something unusual and important might be happening, the detectives arrived with golf clubs and met with Norton at a nearby golf course.

Elder pleaded not guilty to assault with intent to murder and was held in the county jail overnight, since he had been unable to raise the $10,000 bail. Entering jail, he retained his usual confident demeanor. He told the reporters, "I'm not the least bit worried about the outcome of this case. I guess I can endure the inconvenience and embarrassment."

The reporters asked him, "Why should Mr. Norton accuse you of such a serious crime?"

"There is very bitter feeling and animosity between Mr. Norton and myself dating back nearly twenty years."

"Do you think that Mr. Norton was really accosted or is it a dream?"

"I don't think he was accosted. He just made up his mind to cause me some trouble and did it. His mind works very peculiarly, and sometimes I don't think he's responsible for what he does."

With that, Elder entered the jail.

The next day, free on bail, Elder tried to bolster his alibi. He appealed, through the newspapers, for a "fellow lodger" whom he claimed to have met at about 10:00 Tuesday night in the hallway of the Eagle Hotel on his way to the bathroom. Naturally, such a witness would give independent support to Elder's story that he had spent the entire night at the hotel. Without the "fellow lodger's" testimony, the alibi rested solely on Elder and his wife. "I don't know if he saw me," Elder told reporters, "but I'd be tickled to death to have him come forward to help me."

After meeting for several hours with his attorney, the former dean met with the reporters and detailed his version of his activities on Tuesday night. He said he had filled his car with gas at a station near the hotel in the evening and went to bed early with his wife. He woke about "10 or 11 o'clock" to go to the bathroom down the hall. This was when, he said, he had seen the other lodger in the corridor. After that, he said, he had gone back to bed until breakfast time. The police, however, had already told the reporters that the hotel's chambermaid had said that she believed that only one person had slept in the bed in the Elders' room. She based this belief on the state of the bedclothes in the morning when she had gone in to make up the room. Elder had probably already heard about this witness from his lawyer, and he dismissed the story saying, "She must be mistaken. The bedclothes were all ruffled up."

When asked again about Norton's motive in charging him with assault, Elder said, "I know nothing about the motive for Norton's claim, but for some time I haven't had much respect for him, and maybe he feels the same way about me."

The next day, May 29, the state police revealed another witness against Elder: another of Norton's neighbors, Mrs. Edith Weymouth. They said she was being held out of state, for her safety, until her testimony was needed. She had told police that on the previous Tuesday night she had watched from her house—only two doors from the Norton home—as a dark sedan cruised slowly up and down the street five times between dusk and 11:00, when it had parked across the street. The sharp-eyed Mrs. Weymouth, according to police, noticed that the car bore white license plates with green numbers—New Hampshire plates.

Mrs. Weymouth then had gone to visit a neighbor and, on returning, heard sharp voices from the driveway of the Nortons' home. Then she saw a man run to the street, jump into the car, and drive off.

The police also made clear to the press what had been implicit since Elder had been arrested—that they felt he was connected to the Speer murder. They told the newspapermen that they believed the motive of Norton's attacker was to prevent the solution of the murder. They took the additional step, as if to underline the seriousness of their charge, of assigning troopers to guard the campus at Mount Hermon, as well as posting troopers and detectives at Norton's house.

The hearing to determine whether the case would be referred to the grand jury was scheduled for June 3.

The Hearing

The parties and their lawyers appeared before Judge Philip H. Ball, who would determine whether there was sufficient evidence against Elder to refer the case to the grand jury. This hearing was open to the public, unlike the inquest into the Speer murder. It was to be a day of sensational testimony.

Under questioning by Assistant District Attorney Henry Herr, Mr. Norton repeated his story of the assault, adding some details not previously reported. He testified that when he saw the figure approaching him up his driveway, he heard Elder say, "Mr. Norton, I want to talk with you." Norton then approached him and Elder ordered, "Get back into that corner." Norton, though, continued to approach him until Elder said, "You have got to do it." At that point, Norton told the court, "I saw the muzzle of the gun pointing at me about shoulder height, not probably three feet from me. I don't know why it wasn't exploded at that point. I made a further dash and grabbed the knob of the kitchen door and plunged through into the kitchen and still the gun hadn't exploded. I closed the kitchen door, locked it and shouted to Mrs. Norton that Tom Elder was outside with a gun." He described the gun as a small one—with a bore "about the size of a lead pencil."

But it was on cross-examination that those filling the courtroom heard the dramatic revelations they had been hoping for. Elder's lawyer, Charles Fairhurst, first set out to establish that Norton and Elder had long been enemies, although they had worked virtually side by side for more than twenty years. In fact, their offices in Holbrook Hall had been next to one another. Norton testified that differences between himself and Elder had begun in 1922 when he had accused Elder of interfering in the work of the treasurer's office. There were other differences relating to school policy, he said.

It soon became apparent why Fairhurst had bothered to have Norton testify that his office at Mount Hermon had been next to that of Elder. Under his relentless grilling, Norton reluctantly admitted that he had made a hole through the wall in his office's closet in order to watch Elder and his attractive secretary, Miss Evelyn Dill. Norton, obviously embarrassed, acknowledged to Fairhurst that he had observed Elder and Dill at least three times, and he had reported the results of his spying to the then headmaster, Dr. Henry Cutler: "I reported that I saw him kiss her at the desk."

This report, he said, led Dr. Cutler to call a meeting in his study with Dean Elder, Mrs. Elder, and Norton. This meeting ended when Cutler asked all present to kneel in prayer. Fairhurst pressed Norton to agree that he had prayed for God's forgiveness for telling such a story ("And did you ask God to forgive you for being such a miserable skunk?"), but Norton vigorously denied it.

Nevertheless, Norton's basic story of Elder's assault was unshaken. Assistant District Attorney Herr called Yvonne Arsenault, the maid in the house next to Norton's, to testify that she had seen a man wearing a long dark overcoat and carrying a gun in the Nortons' driveway, and she heard him shout, "Hey." The neighbor, Mrs. Edith Weymouth, testified she had heard a sharp voice followed by the sound of an automobile pulling away from the area of the Norton home at "furious speed" about the time of the assault. She also had seen, she said, a car with license plates with a white background driving back and forth on their street as early as 9:00 in the evening.

Fairhurst did not call any witnesses. He and District Attorney David Keedy made brief pleas to the judge—Fairhurst arguing that the charges should be dismissed, and Keedy asking that Elder be held for the grand jury. Judge Ball ruled immediately. "Probably guilty," he said, "held for the grand jury in $10,000 bail."

Elder appeared shaken by this decision, but he was soon cheered to learn that his friends at the Holstein-Friesian Association had voted a fund of $2,000 for his defense. "That was wonderful! This is a great comfort to me," he said. Free on bail, he left the courtroom. The *Times* reported that Elder said to a police officer outside the courtroom, "I am glad this has happened. I hope God gives me strength to see this through."

The Trial

∽

On July 14, the grand jury duly indicted Elder on two counts: assault with intent to murder, and assault with a deadly weapon, putting Norton "in fear of bodily harm." Elder was immediately arraigned. He pleaded not guilty and was released on the same $10,000 bond.

Trial opened on July 22 before Judge Thomas J. Hammond. A jury of twelve men was quickly empaneled and then taken, at the request of District Attorney David Keedy, to view the home of Mr. and Mrs. Norton at 71 Haywood Street, the scene of the alleged assault. When they returned, the jury and the spectators in the crowded courtroom heard Keedy outline the prosecution's case. No witnesses were called that day.

The first witnesses the next day were the policemen who had received Norton's excited telephone call the night of May 25. Keedy also introduced a page of *The Old Farmers' Almanac* to prove that the moon was full on that night. Keedy recognized that he was faced with what lawyers call a "swearing contest" in which the word of Norton was fundamentally the only evidence against Elder, who would strongly deny the story and present an alibi supported by his wife. For that reason he was careful to present as many witnesses and as much evidence beyond the word of Norton as he could.

Taking the witness stand, Norton declined to sit and remained standing throughout the more than one hour of his testimony. He was a large man, with his gray hair parted in the middle, and stood with his hands behind him, rocking slightly from side to side, only occasionally resting his hands on the brass railing at the front of the witness box.

He repeated to the jury his story of the assault. As soon as he heard the assailant say, "Mr. Norton, I want to talk to you," he testified, "I recognized the voice and face as that of Thomas E. Elder." When Elder opened his coat and took out the gun, Keedy asked, "What effect did that have on you?"

"I realized that I was in danger. It put me in terror of my life. I dashed across the garage and grabbed a portion of the door bringing it partially with me, partly in front of me. It was a gun directed at me and I dashed into the vestibule."

On cross-examination, Elder's attorney Fairhurst once again concentrated on the history of the enmity between the two men. Norton readily agreed that over a period of at least ten years while he and Elder had worked in close proximity at Mount Hermon, they had disagreed on a number of issues relating to the school.

"We had had differences over school matters and, I will not deny, on other matters."

Then Fairhurst returned to the specific incident that had caused the sensation at the hearing: Norton's "spying" on Elder and his secretary, Miss Dill, in 1931. Had Norton reported a scene between Elder and Miss Dill to Dr. Cutler?

"Yes."

"Was it something got by spying on him?"

"Yes."

"What was it you reported to Dr. Cutler?"

"I reported having seen him kiss his stenographer and having seen him and his stenographer in each other's embrace."

Norton told how he had drilled a hole through the wall of his office closet, which afforded him a view of Miss Dill's office. He covered the hole, he said, with a piece of cardboard. Then, again prompted by Fairhurst, he repeated his account of the meeting among Dr. Cutler, the Elders, and himself that followed his revelations. The dispute was thrashed out at this meeting, he said, and the meeting ended in a prayer session in which everyone participated. Then Mr. Norton left the stand.

To corroborate Norton's story of the assault, the district attorney called the maid, Yvonne Arsenault, who was employed by Norton's next door neighbor, and Mrs. Edith Weymouth, another neighbor. Miss Arsenault testified that she had seen a man in a long coat with a gun in his hands in the Norton driveway, and Mrs. Weymouth described the automobile bearing New Hampshire license plates driven by that person.

Throughout the prosecutor's case, Elder sat with his counsel, apparently unmoved, making notes and chuckling from time to time.

Also in the courtroom, sitting unobtrusively throughout the trial among the other spectators, was John A. Durham, an assistant Massachusetts attorney general who was still investigating the Speer murder.

On the next day of the trial, the prosecutor called two other witnesses to corroborate Norton's testimony: Mrs. Norton, and Frank King, another neighbor who testified that he had heard a car start and drive away rapidly at about the time Norton claimed to have been assaulted. With that testimony in the record, the prosecution rested.

The defense case, skillfully orchestrated by Fairhurst, began with far more testimony about the "kissing" episode than about the assault or Elder's alibi. Fairhurst's strategy was to suggest to the jury that the personal animosity that Norton felt toward Elder might have been enough to prompt him to make up a story to "get" Elder. In addition, he probably felt that the jurors would react negatively to Norton's spying. It was vital to this strategy—to prevent it from backfiring—that Elder, in his testimony, take the high road and persuade the jury that he held no grudge against Norton.

The first defense witness called by Fairhurst was Richard Watson, long connected with Mount Hermon but now retired and serving as a probation officer in Connecticut. He told the jury that the headmaster at the time of the "kissing incident" was Dr. Henry Cutler and that Cutler had asked Watson to assist him in investigating Norton's charges. Watson and Cutler went to Norton's office in Holbrook Hall, when no one else was in the building, and in a bizarre scene, one sat at Miss Dill's desk and the other peeped through the hole in the wall. Watson testified that when Dr. Cutler sat at Miss Dill's desk, he could see only Cutler's chest and shoulders.

More importantly, Watson testified that after the incident

Norton told him, "I've apologized to Dr. Cutler, I've apologized to Miss Dill; I've apologized to Mr. Elder and now I apologize to you. I would apologize to Mrs. Elder, but he won't let me."

Next, Fairhurst called Dr. Cutler, now age seventy-five. He appeared to be a somewhat reluctant witness, very careful to express himself completely accurately. Describing the meeting among the Elders and Norton in his study, Cutler said that Norton had claimed to have seen Elder "chin-chucking" rather than kissing Miss Dill. Asked, on cross-examination by Keedy about whether he would make "a moral distinction between kissing and chucking," Cutler said, "If I am obliged to make a yes or no answer, I would say yes." But when Keedy asked what the distinction might be, Dr. Cutler admitted he was stumped. "The moral distinction is so narrow that I would not feel competent to define it."

At any rate, Dr. Cutler agreed that Elder was very angry about Norton's accusation. Keedy asked, "There was one time when he [Elder] threatened violence to Mr. Norton over this?" Cutler: "Yes."

Cutler agreed that at the meeting in his study, after Norton had made his charge and Elder had denied it, all knelt in prayer, the burden of which was that "peace and harmony should prevail among the forces at Mount Hermon School."

Keedy also established, through Cutler, that Elder had recently appealed to him for help in obtaining a pension from the school. Cutler said that Elder had claimed to be destitute. Later, Cutler testified, Elder told him he had received a bankbook in the mail, addressed in handwriting he had recognized as Norton's. This testimony was not explained at this point. Later, though, it was made clear that Norton (who had taken a job at the local bank) had learned that Elder had on deposit in the Franklin County Trust Company in Greenfield between $2,500 and $3,000 at the very time that he was claiming destitution. (This was a substantial sum during these Depression years. The average annual per capita income in New Hampshire, where Elder lived, was $571 in 1940, and probably not any higher than that in 1937.) The mailing of the bankbook showing this amount on deposit would have made Elder aware that Norton was in a position to demonstrate that his claim of poverty was false. (Indeed, if Norton had mailed the bankbook to Elder, it would seem to have been at least a threat, if not blackmail.) Perhaps it was this information that Norton was providing to the detectives at the golf course meeting.

Another surprise Keedy revealed, through Cutler's testimony, was a letter sent by Elder to Cutler. Dated July 1, 1935—some nine months after the killing of Elliott Speer, and several months after Elder's resignation—the letter was the only item of evidence that referred in any way to Speer's killing. (Neither side in the case, of course, would have been allowed to suggest to the jury that Elder, the defendant here, had been the primary suspect in the murder of Elliott Speer.) In the letter, Elder, apparently referring to the continuing investigation of the Speer murder, which he felt was aimed at him, complained to Cutler: "I think I am not wrong in believing that Mr. Norton had used the story about Miss Dill he started under your administration. That kind of gossip, contemptible as it is, may have found fertile ground in the gossip-loving brains of some of the investigators as well as in certain types of minds at Mount Hermon."

In the chess match between Keedy and Fairhurst, Keedy seemed to have blunted Fairhurst's efforts to attribute a motive of revenge to Norton, if only by suggesting that Elder had at least as strong a motive to harm Norton. The two white-haired old men obviously disliked each other intensely, but at this point in the trial, Norton's reasons to hurt Elder seemed no stronger than Elder's motives to harm Norton. But Elder was yet to take the stand.

The first witness for the defense, however, was the neat and slim Miss Dill, wearing a conservative but tasteful navy blue outfit. She denied that the former dean had ever acted in an inappropriate way toward her. Specifically, she denied that he had kissed her or chucked her under the chin.

Next, it was Elder's turn. While blaming Norton for having persecuted him in various ways, he nevertheless turned a smile full of Christian forgiveness on his old nemesis. On direct examination by Fairhurst, he traced Norton's dislike for him to an incident many years before when Elder took over some of the duties that Norton's brother had been performing at the school. The brother's job was eventually eliminated. Elder said Norton resented this. Elder added that when he had applied to go to France with the YMCA during the war, Norton had written to some unidentified person alleging that Elder "was not fitted for that kind of work or any other of responsibility."

Elder then described his actions on the night of the alleged assault, including filling his car with gasoline and asking the attendant where he could park overnight. He denied wearing a long coat such as Norton and Miss Arsenault had described Norton's assailant as wearing.

Turning to the meeting in Dr. Cutler's study, at which Norton's accusation that he had seen Elder kissing Miss Dill was aired, Fairhurst had his client describe the scene in detail:

"What did Mr. Norton say?"

"I would say in substance that he said I had laid across the desk and chucked Miss Dill under the chin, or kissed her. I don't remember."

"What did you say?"

"I said it was a damned lie."

"Was that all?"

"I asked Dr. Cutler if he would take the ladies [apparently both Mrs. Cutler and Mrs. Elder were present] outside a minute or two and let me give Mr. Norton a thrashing."

Dr. Cutler apparently declined this invitation and proposed instead that they all pray together. Elder described what followed: "Mr. Norton prayed that he might be forgiven for his habits of spying. I asked God to forgive him also."

Fairhurst turned to the district attorney and said, "Your witness."

Keedy, before getting to the more colorful aspects of the case, had Elder admit that he had been attempting, through Dr. Cutler, to get a retirement allowance from Mount Hermon on the basis that he was destitute.

The prosecutor then turned to the dean's relationship with Miss Dill. Elder admitted that he had taken her on trips to Brattleboro, Vermont, to the offices of the Holstein-Friesian Association, and that he had given her driving lessons. When asked whether he had taken her to the theater in Boston, Elder said he could not remember.

Keedy asked him if he thought that he would have been discharged if the kissing episode had been true. Elder said that he thought he would only have been reprimanded sharply. Keedy appeared incredulous:

"Do you think that only a reprimand was all you deserved if this kissing story had been true?"

"It was indiscreet."

Next, Keedy returned to the now-familiar scene in Dr. Cutler's study:

"You moved toward Mr. Norton when he made his charge against you?"

"I moved in his direction."

"You went toward him with anger in your heart?"

"With indignation."

Keedy willingly joined in the wordplay: "With indignation approaching wrath?"

"But not with vengeance," responded the confident Elder.

"Well, what do you mean when you say you wanted to thrash him? You wanted to strike him, didn't you?"

Elder smiled at his questioner with an air of patient understanding. "I wanted to take him across my knee and spank him like a kid."

Finally, Keedy took the witness through the prayer session:

"And that prayer service, as far as you were concerned, it was a mere sham and mockery, wasn't it?"

"At the beginning it was."

"At the beginning. When did it change?"

"It changed when Mr. Norton prayed to God for forgiveness."

"So then you asked God to forgive him, too?"

"Yes."

"And did you forgive him?"

"Yes."

On redirect examination, Fairhurst dealt with the issue of Elder's efforts to get a pension from Mount Hermon. He read from a letter Elder had written to Dr. Cutler, in which the old dean complained that, "after all my life's work and after I have worn my heart out working for Mount Hermon School," the school now chose "to deal with me as if my life's a failure."

With that, Elder left the witness stand, smiling benignly at Norton, the jury, and the spectators, but not, apparently, at Judge Hammond, who had more than once admonished Elder to answer Keedy's questions, and had even warned him: "and don't make them [the answers] evasive."

Mrs. Elder, following her husband, testified briefly in support of his alibi.

The final defense witness was the aged night clerk at the Eagle Hotel in Keene. Perhaps revealing something of the inner life of apparently staid New Englanders, he testified that he filled his time on duty at the hotel by reading love stories, "one every night." He read a complete one every night, he said, because "I like to get 'em lernt." More to the point, he testified that he was certain that the one man who came into the hotel after midnight on the night of the assault was not Mr. Elder.

Fairhurst announced, "Your honor, the defense rests."

The rebuttal case began with the owner and operator of the gas station in Keene at which Elder had testified he filled up his car the night of the assault. The witness, Russell Batchelder, confirmed that Elder had indeed filled up his automobile at the station, but, importantly, also testified that Elder was wearing a long coat, reaching to his calves, contradicting both Elder and his wife.

The court announced that it would adjourn until the next day, instructed the jury not to discuss the case, and gaveled the day to an end.

Elder left the courtroom and soon caught up with Miss Dill in the corridor. They spoke with easy familiarity, and their conversation, as a reporter observed, "was punctuated with laughter."

The next day was to be the last of the trial. Keedy put Norton on the stand briefly and followed him with Mrs. Nettie Burt, a chambermaid at the Eagle Hotel who testified that in her opinion only one person had slept in the bed of the Elders' room on the night of the assault. With that, Keedy ended the prosecution's case.

In his summation, Fairhurst argued to the jury that Norton had either made a mistake or had purposely sought to injure Elder when he identified him as his assailant: "Does it appeal to your reason, does it appeal to anybody's reason, that this man Elder, who had lived thirty or forty years in these parts, who was known widely, would go out to commit murder on a moonlight night, in his own car, without a disguise, and drive up and down a street waiting for his victim to come home? Does it appeal to reason, that is all I ask."

Keedy also recognized that ultimately the question for the jury was the truthfulness of the two men. He told the jury, "The Commonwealth accepts that issue and fears no comparison you may make between the veracity of Norton and Elder." Keedy turned Elder's earlier description of Norton as having a "Jekyll and Hyde" personality back on the defendant: "Elder is a Jekyll moving through the world with good works by day, and a Hyde taking an inhuman form and doing acts of cruelty by night."

Judge Hammond instructed the jury on the law, and at 4:30 in the afternoon the twelve men retired to begin their deliberations.

More than five hours later, at 9:45, the jury of merchants and farmers returned to the still-crowded courtroom. The court clerk asked the foreman, "What is your verdict on the first count?"

"Not guilty."

"What is your verdict on the second count?"

A pause.

"Not guilty."

Judge Hammond sharply silenced the courtroom, although it was still very quiet.

Elder kissed his wife and enthusiastically shook the hand of Mr. Fairhurst. Mr. and Mrs. Norton had gone home. The clerk told Elder he was discharged from custody, and the judge thanked the jury for their efforts and dismissed them.

The Mount Hermon community was shocked. Norton wrote to Roberts, the secretary of the board of trustees, in early August to express his anger that Watson and Cutler testified for Elder:

> Where is integrity to be found? It makes me sick at heart! I watched Elder & Miss Dill carry on their affairs for months,

even years and many other people at Hermon knew of it too. How Dr. Cutler could have been ignorant of it I can't understand. No one else had the courage to say a word about it. I finally spoke out, convinced it was the right thing to do, but Dr. Cutler wouldn't believe me and wanted me to admit it was all a mistake. So Elder got away with a bit of advice to be a little more careful in his conduct. I don't know whether Dr. Cutler ever told Elliott Speer anything of the Dill matter or not. Elliott never mentioned it to me. The Elder-Dill affair continued all through Elliott's 2 years at Hermon, but I decided I had done my duty. I have an idea he (Elliott) was seeing things, but we'll never know.

I am not convinced that Elder's attack on me was so much on account of the Dill affair as because he feared he was trapped by my knowledge of his bank account,—that I might expose him to Dr. Cutler.

I wonder if anyone feels that this event & trial has brought out anything new as to the Speer case. I think people are more firmly convinced now as to who killed Elliott, but is there any additional evidence because of the recent case?

Robert's reply was supportive but noncommittal. Gradually, the affair was forgotten as the adversaries went back to their lives.

Art and Life

After the verdict there was a brief flurry of articles about the case, but before long the mystery of Elliott Speer's murder and the possible role of Dean Elder once again faded from public view. Over the years since then, there have been occasional newspaper and magazine articles about the crime with titles like "The Headmaster Murder Mystery" and "School for the Perfect Crime." But the murder of Elliott Speer is still unsolved, and it seems destined to remain that way. If this were a mystery novel, all questions would be answered here. But this is not a novel.

The actual mystery novel found in Elliott Speer's library, *The Public School Murder*, which he had recommended to his wife as "a good story," has a number of striking similarities to the real mystery surrounding the death of the real headmaster. Not only is the method of killing virtually the same (shooting the headmaster through the window of his study at night), but the time (September) and the place (a private secondary school) are also the same in the fictional and actual cases.

In the novel, the person who solves the case is the head of the school's board of governors, a businessman. In the case of Elliott Speer's murder, Wilfred Fry, the president of the schools' board of trustees, a businessman, also played a crucial role. He was the first to see the Dear Tom letter and to recognize it as a possible forgery—the first clue to point to Dean Elder.

There was also an inquest in *The Public School Murder,* and it resulted in an unsatisfying result, just as the real inquest in Greenfield did. In the book, though, the inquest was public, and it concluded that the killing had been an accident.

The form of the mystery novel requires that all loose ends be tied up at the end of the book. As a result, most mystery novels do not end with trials. Trials are messy—there are rules of evidence, the requirement of proof beyond a reasonable doubt, and maddeningly unpredictable juries. Mystery novels typically end with the sleuth, usually an amateur, describing in detail the manner in which the crime was committed. The murderer then either confesses or otherwise unequivocally reveals his guilt. *The Public School Murder* is a good example. In the novel, the amateur sleuth has an apparently casual discussion near the end of the book with the narrator and one of the older masters (more or less the second-in-command, like a dean). The conversation turns to the crime, and the chairman (the sleuth) gives a detailed description of how the crime was committed and, more importantly, why. The killer acted, he says—as if speculating—because the headmaster was blackmailing him. In fact, of course, the chairman has seen the blackmail letter, and, of course, he is having this conversation to reveal to the murderer—the old master—that he has been discovered.

Shortly after this, the old master, who now knows that the chairman has solved the crime, commits suicide in such a way that no scandal is attached either to himself or to the school. There is no trial. Only the chairman, the narrator, and the reader know who the killer really was.

It is an entertaining book, and one can easily see why Elliott Speer enjoyed reading it. In addition to the mystery, it is full of comments, mostly unfavorable and tongue-in-cheek, about secondary school students and teachers and about English "public" education.

The mystery of the murder of Elliott Speer illustrates as well as any case could that our legal system and the authorities charged with enforcing the law do not always catch and punish those responsible for serious crimes. Not only is reality inherently messy, but also our legal system is not designed to ensure that every criminal is caught and convicted. On the contrary, it is constructed to ensure that innocent people are not wrongly convicted. We are justly proud, in the abstract, of this bias in our system, but often we are frustrated when real crimes go unsolved, or when real criminals go unpunished.

But although courts are properly restricted by the law with respect to the evidence they can consider and the standards of proof needed to charge and convict a person of a crime, you and I are not so limited. In everyday life, we regularly make decisions based on incomplete evidence, on evidence that would not be admissible in court, and on probabilities. In that spirit, we can examine the evidence available to us—much of which would not be admitted in court—and try to imagine exactly what happened.

A Possible Scenario

Dean Elder is the obvious suspect. The evidence that he forged the Dear Tom letter is convincing, even overwhelming. As District Attorney Bartlett pointed out at the inquest, that letter would have been of no use to Elder as long as Elliott Speer was alive. The dean did not show the letters to Fry, we should remember, until Fry had made it clear that Elder was not to be named acting headmaster. If the trustees had decided differently, it is a good bet that the letters never would have been disclosed and Elder never would have been suspected of the murder.

The other assumption that we will make—contrary to the jury verdict in the 1937 case—is that it was Dean Elder who threatened Mr. Norton with a gun. Of course, we have information that the jury did not have: that Elder had a motive to silence Norton, not about the dean's relationship with Miss Dill, but about Elder's possible murder of Speer. The jurors were not told that Elder had been the chief suspect in the murder of Elliott Speer, or that the police were still seeking more evidence to charge him with the killing. We do not know what information Norton may have had, beyond the fact that the dean had substantial funds on deposit in a bank at the same time he was telling the Mount Hermon authorities that he was destitute. Elder himself may not have known what Norton was telling the police, but he must have felt threatened, even if he only feared that the disclosure of his true financial condition would turn Dr. Cutler against him.

Edwin "Red" Thompson, who was president of the Mount Hermon student council and head of the student disciplinary committee in the school year 1933–1934, had almost daily contact with the dean that year. He recalled that in the late winter and early spring "Mr. Elder's health went down hill so much so that about March of '34, I said to him, 'Dean Elder you look like you have been on a two week drunk. What is the trouble?'" The dean told Thompson that he had been unable to sleep.

Thompson also developed strong opinions about the dean's personality. Although he could be charming and gracious to others, Elder, according to Thompson, was overbearing in his dealings with his family. He insisted that his older son, who was not an athlete, play football at Mount Hermon, and he chose his son's courses at Oberlin College, from which the boy flunked out. Elder then, according to Thompson, brought his son back to Mount Hermon to wash dishes in West Hall, although the son had been happily employed at his uncle's farm.

It is not appropriate to attempt to psychoanalyze the dean from this distance. But we know that he was ambitious. He had expected to be named headmaster when Dr. Cutler finally retired. When Speer was given the job—at the age of thirty-three—Elder saw his hopes dashed. He also must have understood that Speer would replace him in the near future—thus his concern about a pension. He was bitter about his treatment at Mount Hermon, as Wilfred Fry testified at the inquest. And whatever his actual relationship with Miss Dill, it was evidently a subject of discussion and even ridicule on campus. In fact, one former student recalls hearing in the fall of 1933 that Speer had told Elder that Miss Dill "would have to go."

Here then is a possible scenario to explain the letters. The dean in late 1933 raised the issue of a pension with Speer (we know this happened: the chaplain, Lester P. White, testified at the inquest that Speer had told him that he and Elder had been discussing a possible pension and that Elder's idea of the size of his pension was far different from Speer's). Possibly, this issue became a source of contention between the two men. Elder came away from his conversations with Speer understanding not only that he would not receive a generous pension but also that Speer was losing patience with him. Speer may also have mentioned Miss Dill. The dean's bitterness and anger increased over the winter, to such an extent that it affected his health. Unable to sleep, in February he drafted the letters, putting into them everything he wished for—not only a salary increase, pension, free fuel, and the like, but also an imagined relationship in which Speer relied on him for advice (as Dr. Cutler had) and, for good measure, a bit of revenge against Stephen A. Norton.

Moreover, the Dear Tom letter, if Speer were out of the way, could have been used to show the archconservatives among the faculty and alumni that they had been right about Speer all along. The letter would make Speer appear careless and a religious liberal. ("I think you worry too much about the socialistic tendencies of some of the younger teachers. If they do not believe in immortality, I think they should be honest and teach their convictions.") In the Dear Tom letter, Speer admits that he may have been too lax in disciplinary matters ("You may be right in saying I made a mistake in laxity of discipline.") and blithely dismisses the conservatives' demigods, D. L. and Will Moody. ("The Founder and Mr. W. R. are both dead and a new era based on modernistic views is replacing the old.") The Dear Tom letter also, of course, constitutes a ringing endorsement of Elder as Speer's rightful successor. ("You are by far the most progressive of them all and I am going to leave more and more of that side of the work to you. I simply must be away from the school more and more as time passes. I have explicit confidence in you personally and in your ability. There is not a single phase of the work that you cannot handle exactly as well as I.")

Still brooding on the unfairness of his situation, Elder had the letters transcribed on his trips, knowing that if he had it done at the school even Miss Dill would see that the Dear Tom letter was not genuine. This was a step toward murder, since the dean recognized that the letters could be useful only if Speer was dead. He never considered that, after Speer's death, anyone would question the authenticity of the letters. Hence his confusion and his changing stories about the letter when he was challenged by Fry, Grandin, Houghton, and Bartlett. (He probably did not tell Fry that the letters were copies. He certainly did not say anything to him at first to indicate that a portion of the Dear Tom letter had been deleted. At first he said he could not remember where he had had them copied; then he remembered and led the detectives to the stenographers. He first declined to show the letters to Bartlett, and then told him that the Dear Elliott letter was an original and the Dear Tom letter was a copy. That night, in a phone call to Bartlett's home, he told Bartlett that the copy of the Dear Tom letter omitted some material critical of Dr. Cutler. He also had to claim that it was his custom to carry the headmaster's stationery with him when he traveled.)

Over the months after he wrote the letters, the idea of killing Speer took on more and more reality in the dean's mind. After the invitation of the socialist Norman Thomas to speak at the commencement in June 1934 and the resulting outcry from the conservative alumni, he may have felt that Speer's star was no longer rising, and even that the elimination of the young liberalizer from the scene might be welcomed. Surely, he believed, his subsequent promotion would be universally recognized as appropriate.

He may have thought about murdering Speer in the spring. He may even have watched the headmaster through the window in his study in the evenings. But the campus was crowded with students in the spring, the sun set later and later each day, and the chance of being seen was too great. He had the summer vacation to plan the murder. He could purchase buckshot anonymously on his travels, even purchase a 12-gauge shotgun if he did not already have one. He may have believed that murdering the headmaster shortly before the beginning of the new school year would force the trustees to name him acting headmaster—there would be no time for a search for a new headmaster before the term began—and then he could prove his worth to the board that had so unjustly passed him over two years before.

Speer did not return to campus until September 9. This gave Elder a short window of opportunity. Clearly, the murder would have to be accomplished before the students returned and the campus filled with possible witnesses. To some degree, in fact, the dean was able to control the time when the students and faculty returned to campus. In a letter dated September 4, 1934, from Elder to Speer (addressed "Keemaydin, Timagami, Ontario, Canada"), he wrote, "I have written to the heads of the dormitories, asking them to be sure to return by Saturday, September 15. . . . I am asking the officers to return on Sunday, the 16th, . . . I am asking all other teachers to return here on Monday."

Possibly the dean observed Ford Cottage on several nights before the 14th, with the shotgun in the car, until, on that night he saw his chance. Every day he delayed meant more people on campus, more people to see him. On this evening, the excuse of taking the car to get its headlight repaired, which a witness (other than Mrs. Elder) had heard, would serve to explain why Elder did not arrive at Holbrook Hall immediately after leaving his home.

The drive to Ford Cottage from his house would have taken only a minute or two. He fired the shot between 8:15 and 8:20, walked quickly to his car, and drove to Morgan's Garage, a drive of only two and a half miles, arriving there before 8:30. He may have thrown the gun off the bridge into the Connecticut River or kept it in the car, planning to dispose of it later. When the headlight had been replaced, he drove back to Holbrook Hall and entered inconspicuously, waiting for the call from Ford Cottage that would tell him if he had been successful in eliminating his rival.

What the Law Could Not Do

We asked at the beginning of this book why Elliott Speer had been killed and why no charges were ever brought against anyone for the killing.

Despite the fact that everyone learns in high school about our legal system, with its requirement of proof beyond a reasonable doubt and the presumption of innocence, many are puzzled, even outraged, when the system does not solve a crime and punish the criminal.

This case was no exception. The big-city newspapers pointed their editorial fingers at the relationships among the judges and lawyers involved in the Speer inquest and the Elder assault trial. For example, Charles Fairhurst, Elder's defense attorney, was also chairman of the county Board of Selectmen that had authority over the police. The assistant district attorney in 1937, Henry Herr, who represented the prosecution in the preliminary hearing in the Elder assault case, was a partner in a law firm with Timothy Hayes, the judge who had presided at the inquest. Judge Ball, who heard the testimony at the preliminary hearing on the assault charge and ordered that the case be presented to a grand jury, was a partner with the former district attorney Bartlett.

However, while it was and is unusual in New York and Boston for the lawyers and judges in any given case to be so closely related professionally, the situation in Greenfield was and still is typical of small-town justice in the United States. It is quite natural for the small group of legal professionals in any small town to be members of the same service organizations and to move in and out of the judiciary. There is no reason to believe that this situation prevented the indictment or conviction of anyone in this case.

But why was Dean Elder acquitted in the 1937 assault case? Possibly the jurors were offended by Norton's spying through his "peek hole" on Elder and his secretary, or by his using what he learned working at the local bank to prevent the old dean from obtaining a pension from Mount Hermon. While both Norton and Elder had long associations with the area, it may be that the jury felt that a "not guilty" verdict would strike a middle ground and avoid harming the reputation of either man. They may have been influenced by Dr. Cutler's appearance as a witness for Dean Elder—even though Cutler seemed to have had a difficult time testifying. (In this connection, it should be remembered that Cutler's biography describes Elder as "brilliant but unstable" and as "a disruptive and discordant influence.") Cutler's biographer notes, "The testimony Cutler presented appeared to favor Elder, and the general sentiment was that his very presence, which naturally drew the respect of the court, was a decisive factor in the final outcome. Feeling ran high. Both men involved in the trial had been Cutler's friends, and he had been careful, he thought, to present only the most objective evidence. What angered his acquaintances in North-field and Mount Hermon, was his unwillingness to denounce the man whom they were convinced was a scoundrel."

Or, the jury may simply have believed Elder and his wife and disbelieved Norton—at least enough to justify a verdict for Elder on the basis that the assault had not been proved "beyond a reasonable doubt."

So, we come back to the facts that real life is messier than the world described by mystery novels, and that our legal system is intentionally designed to make it difficult to convict people charged with crimes.

At the first memorial service for Elliott Speer on the Sunday after the murder, at Ford Cottage, Chaplain Lester White chose to read a portion of Paul's letter to the Romans, in which the weakness of human institutions ("the law") is contrasted with the power of God: "For what the law could not do, in that it was weak through the flesh, God sending his own son in the likeness of sinful flesh, and for sin, condemned sin in the flesh." Perhaps the thoughtful chaplain already had the presentiment that human law would fail in this case.

And perhaps Dean Elder, seated among his mourning colleagues listening to the reading, was putting his faith in that very weakness of human law, and his hope in the nonexistence of divine justice.

12

Epilogue

What happened to the people and institutions involved in the Speer case after the murder and the investigations?

Wilfred W. Fry was already dying of cancer, although he might not have known it, by the end of 1934. The president of the board of trustees was the first person to whom Dean Elder showed the Dear Tom letter, and Fry finally decided he had to turn the letters over to the investigators. Fry was president of the Philadelphia advertising firm N. W. Ayer & Son. He was known, as noted before, for "his great honesty and integrity, his unfailing courtesy, his kindness and consideration for those about him."

It is typical of him that, when Thomas Elder was asked by the trustees to retire, and would therefore have to pay tuition if his younger son were to continue his studies at Mount Hermon, Fry wrote Elder, "In view of the fact that your removal from the campus will, as I understand it, involve extra expense in behalf of your son who is a student at Mount Hermon, I should like, if you will permit me, to have his term bills now due and for the remainder of the year, sent to me personally."

Fry and his wife were quiet but generous benefactors of both the Mount Hermon and Northfield schools, giving money particularly to refurbish the chapels at each campus. Letters in the school's archives from Fry to David Porter and others show his love for the school and, as his signature weakened over time, graphically demonstrate the progress of the disease. Wilfred Fry died on July 27, 1936.

David R. Porter was named headmaster after having headed the committee on administration formed following Elliott Speer's murder. Like many of the leaders of the school in this period, he had been closely involved with the YMCA. As headmaster of Mount Hermon, he retained the changes initiated by Elliott Speer and continued to improve the academic standards of the school. He was not an innovator. The trustees decided in 1943 that more progressive leadership was required, and Porter, always modest and courteous, accepted the decision and stepped down. In 1960, he wrote a book, *The Quest of the Best in Education,* which he dedicated to, among others, the "masters at Mount Hermon School." He returned to service with the YMCA but remained close to the school until his death.

Robert E. Speer was active in the investigation of his son's murder (examining his diaries, helping to search for the murder weapon, and testifying at the inquest on the inauthenticity of the Dear Tom letter), but ultimately he returned to his writing and preaching. He had been instrumental in forming the predecessor of the National Council of Churches and maintained close ties to the Presbyterian Church. He always preached against capital punishment and said, "I would far rather the murder of my son go unsolved than that anyone should ever suffer capital punishment for his murder." Dr. Speer died in November, 1947.

Charlotte "Holly" Speer went on after her husband's murder to have a distinguished career as an educator. She became head-mistress of the Ethel Walker School, a secondary school for girls in Simsbury, Connecticut. She was regarded by her many friends as gracious and kind, but was not afraid to stand up for her princi-ples. She resigned from Ethel Walker (despite the fact that she had three daughters to support) when the owner of the school refused to discontinue the practice of purchasing heating oil on the black market. She then became headmistress of the Masters

School, another secondary school for girls, in Dobbs Ferry, New York. She raised her three daughters, who still live in New England, and remained a lifelong friend of Sophie Birdsall. She died in 1976.

Thomas Elder retired to a poultry farm in Alton, New Hampshire, after leaving Mount Hermon. He continued his association with the Holstein-Friesian Association and was classifying cattle at a New Jersey dairy farm when he died in September 1948. A friend who was with him when he died wrote, "If anyone anywhere ever thought ill of Tom Elder, they should have seen him in his last moments. He was at peace with the Almighty." There is a story that he had told many people that he had left a letter with his attorney that was to be opened only after his death. As Elder certainly anticipated, this caused many to think that the letter would contain a post-deathbed confession. In fact, the letter simply dealt with his desires with respect to his burial. No doubt the speculation about the letter amused the old dean.

Mount Hermon School for Boys, as Elliott Speer had foreseen, has continued to change and adapt to modern times. In 1971 Mount Hermon and the Northfield School for Girls (the "Seminary" name had long since been dropped) merged, creating one school. The work program still exists, though it is somewhat reduced. Work assignments on the farm are highly sought after by today's students. Young men and women come to Northfield Mount Hermon (as it is now called) from all over the world and from every possible religious background. Chapel is no longer mandatory, though small groups of students meet with (or without) faculty advisors to worship in their own traditions. More than 40 percent of students receive financial aid. The student population is far more diverse than at any time in the past.

Elliott Speer's name and influence are visible at the schools today. In 1984, at the fiftieth reunion of the class of 1934, a group was formed to ensure that the murdered headmaster should be memorialized in an appropriate way. This group became known as "the Speer boys," ironically in view of Elliott Speer's practice of referring to his students, and treating them, as "men." It later included members of the classes of 1933 to 1936. With a goal of creating a fund of $100,000 to be used at the discretion of the headmaster for emergency needs of students and faculty and for activities that would broaden the students' educational experience, the Speer boys vastly exceeded their aims. By 1999, the fund reached nearly half a million dollars. In addition, the group created a lounge for the students named for Elliott Speer and raised a granite monument to him on the walkway between Ford Cottage and West Hall. The inscription on the monument reads:

ELLIOTT SPEER 1898–1934

HEADMASTER 1932–1934

Innovative and beloved leader, he changed and
invigorated Mount Hermon by enlivening the
academic and social life of the school and by
introducing interscholastic athletics. He was
always an inspiring presence to students in his
office, in his home, and on the campus.
This memorial stands as a tribute to the
values he kindled in his students during
his brief tenure as headmaster and as a
reminder to present and future students of
the legacy of Elliott Speer.

Notes

Prologue: *The Key to Heaven*
Some of this material, obviously including descriptions of what some of the characters were thinking, is my speculation. The event, though, is recounted in the
school newspaper, *The Hermonite* (November 5, 1932).

Chapter 1: *Murder at Ford Cottage*
Sources for the description of the evening of the shooting are primarily the *New
York Times* articles beginning on September 15, 1934, and the inquest testimony
of Holly Speer, David and Sophie Birdsall, Mr. Welles, Daniel Bodley, William
Dierig, Dr. Stetson, the medical examiner, and Charles Van Amburgh, the fire-
arms expert for the Massachusetts State Police.

Chapter 2: *Mount Hermon from Moody to Speer*
Sources for this chapter include the *New York Times;* an October 1977 *Yankee*
magazine article entitled "The Study of a Murder," by Burnham Carter (p. 102);
and an August 1939 *American Mercury* article entitled "The Headmaster Murder
Mystery," by Harland Manchester (p. 410). Other facts are from Burnham Carter's history of the Northfield Schools, *So Much to Learn* (Northfield Mount Hermon School, 1976). The letter describing the dire consequences of modern
dancing is quoted from this book. The material on D. L. Moody is from Carter's
book and from George M. Marsden, *Fundamentalism and American Culture* (Ox-
ford University Press, 1980). The observations about Cutler's regime and the
changes initiated by Elliott Speer are from an insightful unpublished manuscript
in the school archives, "Religion at Northfield Mount Hermon—A History," by
William Compton, a retired Mount Hermon faculty member. The statement by
Bill Morrow is from "Bill Morrow's Reminiscences," published (apparently in
1985) in *The* (Northfield Mount Hermon School) *News*. In addition, I am im-
mensely indebted to Dr. William Cole, S. Prestley Blake, and Edwin "Red"
Thompson for sharing their memories of Mount Hermon during Elliott Speer's
time. The Bible quotation is from the King James Version.

Chapter 3: *Elliott Speer*
Sources for this chapter include Dr. Robert Speer's eulogy for his son, delivered
in November 1934, Carter's *So Much to Learn,* the *Scotsman,* October 19, 1934,
and a letter (in the school archives) from Richard Birdsall, the son of David Birdsall, Elliott Speer's friend. Frederick Lewis Allen's wonderful *Only Yesterday: An*

Informal History of the 1920's (Perennial Classics, 2000) and David F. Burg's *The Great Depression: An Eyewitness History* (Facts on File, 1996) provided background on the stock market crash and its aftermath. I am again indebted for anecdotes about Elliott Speer at Mount Hermon to Dr. William Cole, Edwin Thompson, S. Prestley Blake, Caroline Speer Fisher, and the anonymous writer of the final anecdote (which is in the school archives, and to which I have made some slight corrections).

Chapter 4: The Police Investigation
Sources for this chapter include the *New York Times* and *Newsweek* and *Time* magazine articles. (Lieutenant Dasey's name is sometimes spelled "Dacey" in the papers. I have adopted the spelling used in the transcript of the inquest as more likely correct.) Sources for the daily progress of the investigation also include the inquest testimony of Fry, Grandin, and Bartlett. The material about Stokes and the Millen murders is from *New York Times* articles in February and March 1934. Biographical material about Wilfred Fry (here and in the next chapter) is from his obituary in the *New York Times* and from Ralph M. Hower, *The History of an Advertising Agency, N. W. Ayer & Son at Work, 1869–1949* (Harvard University Press, 1949). The quotation about not accepting liquor advertising is from the *Christian Century* magazine, September 13, 1933 (p. 1133). The source for the Elder biographical material is the series of *New York Times* articles detailing the 1937 charges and trial relating to Norton and Elder. Porter's article on football is in the September 1911 *Educational Review* (vol. 42, no. 2, p. 162). The information on the fumble return for a touchdown against Harvard (in 1902) is from an unsigned typescript entitled "The Man Who Surprised Harvard and Captured English University Men" in the school archives. The reasons for the trustees' decision not to appoint Elder as acting headmaster are from Fry's inquest testimony. The Bible reading from the memorial service is from the King James Version.

Chapter 5: Dear Elliott and Dear Tom
The material on Fry's acquisition of the letters, his thoughts about them, and his investigation prompted by them, comes primarily from his inquest testimony. The information about Houghton in the Secret Service is from Michael Dorman, *The Secret Service Story* (Delacorte Press, 1967). The background material on Grandin's business activities comes from Grandin's obituary in the *Boston Herald*, December 3, 1968. Bartlett's and Grandin's inquest testimony provide the basis for the rest of the chapter.

Chapter 6: Pressuring the Suspect
This chapter is derived from the inquest testimony. The November 1934 letter concerning communists in the schools is in the Northfield Mount Hermon School archives.

Chapter 7: The Inquest
As is apparent, this chapter, too, is based on the inquest testimony. The information about "King" Watson was kindly provided by Dr. William Cole of the class

of 1935. I am also grateful to Dick Gale for the description of the school's black-smith, Daniel Van Valkenburgh. Quotations from Judge Hayes's report are primarily from the *Boston Evening Globe*, January 9, 1935.

Chapter 8: Was Judge Hayes Right?
The newsreel footage in which District Attorney Bartlett appears was produced by Pathé News. The film, as well as a video version of it, is in the school archives.

Chapter 9: Watching the Dean, 1934–1937
As noted in the text, the wiretap notes, tracings of envelopes to and from the dean's residence, Cutler's letter reporting on his investigation, and a copy of Bartlett's letter to Houghton are in the school's archives at Northfield. Richard Day's biography of Cutler, which is quoted in the text, was very helpful in providing insight into Dr. Cutler's attitude toward Elder after the murder. The description of the meeting between Dr. Cutler and Dean Elder is from a memorandum dated November 26, 1936, from Lieutenant-Detective Maurice Nelligan of the Massachusetts State Police to Stokes, in the school archives.

Chapter 10: "Norton, I want to talk to you"
Newspaper stories, particularly from the *New York Times*, as well as coverage in *Newsweek* and *Time* magazines and the transcript of the preliminary hearing (which is in the school archives), provided the material for this chapter. There apparently is no transcript of the trial itself, as opposed to the hearing. The figure for average per capita income in New Hampshire for 1940 is from *Historical Statistics of the United States, Colonial Times to 1970, Bicentennial Edition*, Part 1 (U.S. Department of Commerce, 1975), p. 244.

Chapter 11: Art and Life
The Public School Murder by R. C. Woodthorpe (Ivor Nicholson & Watson, London, 1932) has been long out of print, but it is worth looking for in libraries. Magazine and newspaper articles dealing with the murder of Elliott Speer include the two magazine articles given in notes to Chapter 2, as well as "Who Murdered Dr. Speer?" in the October 1959 *Yankee* magazine (p. 32), and "Who Killed Elliott Speer" in the April–May 1983 *Country Side* magazine (p. 40). More recently, one Curt Norris authored a syndicated article about the mystery, "School for the Perfect Crime," published in the *Attleboro-North Attleboro (Mass.) Sun Chronicle*, March 11, 2001.

Chapter 12: Epilogue
The material on Wilfred Fry comes primarily from the publications cited in the notes for Chapter 3 and from letters in the school archives. *So Much to Learn*, cited in notes to Chapter 2, is the source for the information about David Porter, which is supplemented by material from interviews with former students, particularly Dr. William Cole. Obituaries in the *Christian Century* (December 10, 1947) and the *New York Times* (November 25, 1947) provided the information concerning Robert E. Speer, except for the quotation about capital punishment, which is

from a letter to the author from Edwin "Red" Thompson. Charlotte "Holly" Speer's obituary in the *New York Times* (November 10, 1976) provided information about her life, as did telephone conversations with her daughter Caroline. Information about changes in the school come from *So Much to Learn,* as well as from an interview with Brian Cavell, director of the work program.

Index

❦

THIS BOOK BELONGS TO THE
VAN BUREN PUBLIC LIBRARY